SPELLING:
Caught or Taught?

SPELLING:
Caught or Taught?

A New Look

Margaret L. Peters

First published in 1967
This revised edition first published in 1985 by
Routledge & Kegan Paul plc

Reprinted 1988, 1992, 1994 by Routledge
11 New Fetter Lane, London EC4P 4EE
29 West 35th Street, New York, NY 10001

Typeset in 10 on 12 point Palatino by
Kelly Typesetting Ltd, Bradford-on-Avon, Wiltshire
Printed and bound in Great Britain by The Guernsey Press

British Library Cataloguing in Publication Data
A catalogue record for this book is available from the British Library

Library of Congress Cataloging in Publication Data
A catalog record for this book is available from the Library of Congress

ISBN 0-415-02762-4

Contents

Contents

1

The spelling problem

In the 1960s most primary school teachers thought that spelling occurred incidentally when children wrote about their interests. Phrases such as 'when the need arises', 'association of ideas' appeared. There was conviction that spelling was a means to an end, and that it should only be a servant of 'creative writing'. There was little evidence of actual instruction in spelling and when instruction did occur it was very often left to individual teachers or even to children themselves to work out a strategy of learning, 'falling back' as Mackay, Thompson and Schaub (1978, p. 131) put it, 'on random procedures and on rote learning'.

In the 1980s teachers' attitudes are changing – on all sides they appeal for help in the teaching of spelling, and in the diagnosis and remediation of spelling difficulties, and this is seen in their demand for courses on the teaching of spelling. All this points to the dilemma in which teachers have been placed in relation to the teaching of spelling.

The dilemma has arisen because, though it is generally agreed that children must be taught to *read*, it has long been assumed that spelling is *caught*, that it occurs incidentally, and if it doesn't, there is very little teachers can do about it. This feeling has also been perpetuated in the last decade or two, by the intriguing but nebulous concept of 'inventive spelling'. This is a concept familiar to teachers who sensibly encourage children to 'have a try', for, by having a 'try', backed up as we shall see later by happy experiences with books, children do 'catch spelling'. But, as teachers know, not all children 'catch'

1

it. Of course, the wise teacher will view and make use of 'invented spelling' not only as a way in to spelling. What are often called 'shifts to conventional spelling' are going to need the teacher 'in interaction with the young writer' (Clay 1983, p. 263) and the teacher needs to know when and, more importantly, *how* to interact. Indeed 'the purpose of invented spelling is to separate the specific problem of learning to spell from the other more satisfying matter perhaps of getting on with writing' (Smith 1982, p. 187).

Many teachers feel deeply, if obscurely, that spelling has some importance although they are not quite sure what. Those who comfort themselves with the feeling that spelling can be picked up incidentally while attending to more important things like 'creative' writing, have not examined whether spelling is picked up in this way, or to what extent. They also have rather an undifferentiated view of learning and do not sufficiently appreciate that different things have to be learnt in different ways. Obviously talk of insight and discovery applies to the learning of things like mathematics and science, and in modern educational theory there has been much more concentration on discovery learning than on the learning of skills, the importance of which has been rather neglected. In learning a skill like spelling, practice, and in particular practice in handwriting, is of cardinal importance, and talk about insight and discovery has very little point when confronted with the anomalies of English spelling, in which words at first sight do not apparently conform to any known principle. The learning of skills, however, is obviously not *just* a matter of practice; for there are other very important factors as well which will be discussed later.

Much of this book will be concerned with the factual question of the extent to which a skill such as spelling can be caught and the extent to which what is caught by some can in fact be taught to those who haven't caught it. Before embarking, however, on the examination of this sort of question a few preliminary remarks must be made about the case for teaching spelling at all. It may well be the case that there are good reasons for learning to spell which the traditional teacher never bothered to make explicit. It may also be the case that there is something to be said for lessons of a formal type in teaching this as well as other skills, which must supplement other more informal ways of handing them on.

What then are the reasons for learning to spell correctly?

The case for good spelling

Obviously, if there were not very good reasons for spelling correctly, the question of spelling would not be one to which parents or teachers give so much attention. Still less would it be a suitable subject for a book such as this. What then are these good reasons?

1 First of all there are reasons connected with communication and consideration for others. If spelling is poor and careless, communication suffers; for either the reader is constantly held up through having to puzzle out what a word is, or else is positively misinformed. The degree of precision necessary in spelling is obviously closely connected with ease and smoothness of communication.

2 There is the connected question of courtesy. Not to speak clearly, not to write legibly and not to spell correctly are marks of discourtesy. Bad spelling is just as bad in this respect as mumbling over a telephone.

3 There is the question of habit-formation. Spelling is a skill in which it is necessary to be precise, and precision generally is one of the main virtues educated people have to acquire. Precision is not only important from the point of view of the other person – the person who is going to receive the communication and read what is written – but also from the point of view of the person who wishes to communicate. The presumption is that some transfer of training occurs, and that what is transferred in a skill such as spelling is not a technique but a habit of care. A casual attitude manifests itself in handwriting, in punctuation, in spelling, and in poorly constructed sentences and paragraphs. Careful attention

to any one of these aspects of writing may well affect the others.

4   An important case for good spelling is that it contributes very effectively to a child's self-concept. It not only gives him status but also the knowledge that he can communicate adequately and acceptably in writing.

When one considers that spelling is a skill that, more than any other, demonstrates to others the existence in a child of an 'easy competence' and is hence a 'status symbol', it is incredible that we do not make more effort to make it available to children particularly those with learning difficulties. For these children are often orally inarticulate, since they are not facile in predicting the end of their own utterances as they speak, or the utterances of others as they listen. These are children hesitant in reading, since inability to predict forthcoming words inhibits their flow in reading. But that is another story.

When these children come to write, their sentences will be short, terse, uncomplicated. 'I went to the zoo.' 'My cat had three kittens. My dad killed two kittens.' 'I work at the Co-op. I put packets out'. These are the kind of offerings made in the traditional 'diary', bland unadorned statements made without fire or even feeling. There are even more pale and uninteresting offerings when children are writing answers to questions in English exercises, however smartly presented in 'kit' form these may be. But that again is another story.

This is bound to be so when children are just expected to write. For it is only when writing is purposeful, when a child has to write to get a message across to someone (in other words, has an audience) that he writes with feeling, colour and strength. And then the sentences may well become less terse, less simple, less unrefined. A boy left a note for his mother, 'Fech Richard and Gary because they mist bus.' A thirty-year-old adult illiterate wrote 'I do not like to see my mother cry'.

Such purposeful writing falls mainly into one of two categories. The first is the category of command, the second of emotional expression. Purposeful writing depends upon strength of feeling, which is certainly not the generator of

4

those bland statements we find in school writing books. And it is purposeful writing and only purposeful writing that we undertake as adults. We write because, and often only if, we must. But when we do write, our writing may betray us as inadequate; it may indicate some hidden competence. Then the reader comments 'He gets his message across!' or 'He can express himself on paper' or merely 'Thanks!' The writer is positively reinforced in a way he cannot be in speaking, which is the other verbally productive skill of which he is capable. But he is going to receive such positive reinforcement *only if* his spelling is adequate. For the skill, or rather sub-skill, relevant to the above is spelling.

5   Another important reason for learning to spell is that nearly all of us can read, and the text we read is, unlike the spoken word, 'petrified'. It doesn't change, because we have through the years internalised it so effectively. Most of us can spell and would resist any attempt at spelling reform just because the spelling system is so deeply embedded within us. The point is that because spelling has become 'petrified' it has to be learned.

6   There is another educationally very important reason for good spelling which is connected with freedom to write. In the 1960s the vogue was for 'creative writing', and it was so strong that when the writer explored teachers' attitudes to children's free writing, it was vividness, speed and quantity of output that mattered to teachers, with relatively little concern for spelling, grammar, punctuation and handwriting. Yet it is only when we have achieved that machine-like spelling of which Schonell spoke (1942), spelling that is automatic, predictable, and infallible, that we are really free to write with confidence, with no backward glances to see if a word 'looks right', and with no offering of a less precise synonym or phrase because the right one is difficult to spell. The competent and hence confident speller will explore with new words, which up till now may have been passive. The new words tentatively tried out in conversation are becoming active. For the competent and confident speller these words will become active on

paper, for he, accustomed to the likelihood of certain sequences of letters in English, will, from his experience in handling such sequences, make a confident and fairly accurate attempt. But the poor speller may avoid using the new and exciting word. He may use a simpler and less precise circumlocution.

Far from being free to write 'excitingly' by ignoring spelling and similar conventions, some children, and adults, are only freed to write when they have learnt to spell correctly. It is like a pianist who can only interpret the music when he knows it 'by heart'. Only when he has reached the stage of muscular recall, and no longer has to go via the medium of visual recognition, only when he is unworried by the intricacies of the written score or by the technicalities of fingering, and the fingers move in sequence, can he attend not to the symbols but to the sound that emerges. In the same way the writer unworried by the intricacies of spelling, can write as freely as he can speak, can expand his ideas, can give examples and figures of speech, confidently and adventurously.

As William James said before the turn of the century, 'The more of the details of our daily life we can hand over to the effortless custody of automatism, the more our higher powers of mind will be set free for their own proper work (1892, p. 67). How true this is of writing.

This sort of freedom in writing is a necessary condition of academic education, one indication among many that a child can profitably proceed with it. In a school where the organisation is a kind of 'banding' or 'setting', this can have important consequences; for, other things being equal, a child who spells correctly and can attend to the content of what he is writing is more likely to achieve promotion to a higher set than one whose teacher, often unintentionally, raises her eyebrows at poor spelling before she can attend to the content. An example of this was an eleven-year-old boy, a very unco-operative and aggressive non-reader, who had been referred at the age of nine. By the age of ten he was reading competently but his spelling was largely random. He was given a year's intensive course in remedial spelling and when he entered the second-ary school he was put in an 'A' stream. This was entirely because he wrote so 'interestingly' and the readers were not distracted by poor spelling. He achieved an impressive array of 'O' levels including a grade I in English language, three 'A' levels with an 'A' and distinction in physics, read physics at the university and proceeded to higher degrees and a distin-guished career in research. As Douglas (1964) showed in the days of streaming, educational advantage and opportunity was strongly influenced by the stream in which a child was placed. It is certain that without efficient spelling this boy would not have qualified for, or maintained his place in the 'A' stream, since he would not have achieved the freedom to write unhampered by spelling problems. Many children, however, never achieve this freedom, and as adults escape somehow from revealing their ineptitude. They may write simply; they may avoid the words they use in everyday speech, because these are too difficult to spell; they may not write at all.

What is involved in spelling?

Why does a poor speller have to go to such lengths? What is preventing him from writing as surely and accurately as the good speller? Consider the case of a ten-year-old writing a 'thank-you letter' for a present: 'Thank you very much for the lovely . . .' All is well up to now. The child has met and used, first passively, then actively, all these words. But now he is faced with the new word. The present he has received is a toy flying saucer. He may avoid writing it by saying 'present' which he can spell. He may offer 'space-ship' which he can attempt. He may try the word itself. Of 967 ten-year-olds attempting the word 'saucer', 462 children wrote it success-fully. The remaining 505 offered between them 209 alternative spellings. If they had been presented with the word saucer to *read*, it would have been read correctly, according to Andrews' norms (1964) of Schonell's Graded Word Reading Test, by 71 per cent of eight-year-olds, and this in a word-reading test, where the words are divorced from the context. Asked to write it, only 47 per cent of ten-year-olds were able to write it correctly. To read a word we look at it and if we do not immediately recognise its pattern as 'saucer', we isolate it into learned phonic elements, s-au-ce-r, which we say, and the meaning *hits* us as we read it in the context of the sentence, provided, that is, that we have heard, or better still used the word before. Reading is from the unknown via the context to the known. Spelling is from the known to the unknown. How can we make this unknown known?

To spell 'saucer' we hear it, or image it aurally or with articulatory movements, sub-vocally, and then we are faced with the many and various combinations, particularly of vowels, that are possible alternatives; aw, or, oo, ough, augh, ser, cer, sa, sir. The alternatives demanded in the complicated competitions devised by detergent and cereal companies are not as puzzling as the alternatives presented in writing an unknown word. They at least offer clues however remote and misleading. Many words to be spelt offer none.

If clues are given in an unknown word that has to be spelt, they are given in the sound, but the same sound can be written in many ways. The known meaningful sound has to be written in an unknown way. In reading, the child or less competent reader is concerned with what a word sounds like. The unknown word is being transformed into the known meaningful sound, that is decoding. Spelling, unlike reading, is encoding a familiar and meaningful sound into a strange and unpredictable code. This is the difference Reid and Donaldson (1979) highlight when they emphasize that phonics for reading is not the same as phonics for spelling. As long as we cling to the sound of the message rather than the code, in other words the sounds comprising the word, not the elements of the code, we cannot possibly write the word in code. It would be safe and reliable if the English language were entirely and un-exceptionally grapho-phonemically regular, that is if every speech sound were always matched with the same written sequence in one-to-one correspondence. The English language is largely but not wholly grapho-phonemically regular.

It is for this reason that research workers have tried to assess how regular indeed it is. In 1953 Hanna and Moore, analysing the regular phonemes (the smallest unit of representation used in alphabet writing – the irreducible meaningful speech sound) in children's speech and writing found that 80 per cent were represented by regular spelling. Groff (1961), looking at the New Iowa Spelling Scale (Greene 1954) which was constructed from the written communications of adults and children, put the percentage at 70 per cent. From a study of words used by children themselves in the course of their writing as collected by Edwards and Gibbon (1964) it looked as if as many as 90 per cent of the words they use are graphophonemically regular. Albrow (1972) described the whole writing system as regular, involving different interlocking conventions. However, Flesch (1983) working on the Hanna *et al.* (1971) computerised list of decodable words, now puts it at 97.4 per cent exactly! So for practical purposes it looks as if between 1 and 3 words in every 10 are grapho-phonemically irregular. Simply to transfer our knowledge of sounds to spelling, would be fatal with the 10–30 per cent of graphophonemically irregular words – so too with the many regular words that could have quite reasonable alternatives, e.g. 'stayed' could reasonably be written 'staid' or 'stade'; 'great' could well be 'grate' or 'grait'.

The only reason that any of us ever get beyond the precariousness of such coding is that we have learned to look attentively and selectively. As humans, sight is our preferred sense; we rely on looking to check almost everything we do. We certainly rely on looking to check the correctness or incorrectness of our spelling. The boy mentioned above was over the last fence when he said, 'Lemme write it down and see what it looks like!' He had, by this time, learnt the look of the most likely sequences of letters in our language. If, for example, we know that in the word 'avenue', the 'n' is followed by 'ue' we are prepared by our knowledge of precedent to write 'ue' in the word 'continue' and not just finish with 'u'. From our knowledge of precedent we implicitly associate structurally similar words. This is because the probability of words conforming to spelling precedent is very high, and it is by becoming familiar with spelling precedents that we become good spellers. In other words, familiarity with a coding system is half the battle in learning to spell.

Wallach (1963), investigating the coding system by which children learn to spell, presented good and poor eleven-year-old spellers with briefly exposed flash cards, and asked them to write what they saw. Some flash cards bore random strings of six letters, e.g. DNEHPS or GWDNML. Some were groups of letters that were very similar to English words, such as APHYST or TERVIC. These can be evolved in party-game manner by one person thinking of a word but only divulging three consecutive letters, e.g. TER. The next person thinks of a word including TER but adds a letter and drops the first, offering ERV and so on

winTER
intERVal
serRVIce
VICtory

producing a nonsense word that reflects the probability structure of English very closely. Indeed, apart from the important fact that it is not derived etymologically, such a word could easily have been an English word.

The experiment revealed that for random words there was very little difference between good and poor spellers, but good spellers were found to recognise nonsense words resembling English much more readily than poor spellers. The good spellers had learned a general coding system based on the probabilities of letters occurring in certain sequences in English. As Frith pointed out (1980), good spellers are in remarkable agreement as to what they consider the correct spelling of nonsense words to be.

This is the case in any language, though there is no transfer from one language to another, because of the difference in the spelling conventions from one language to another. Bruner (1953) quotes an experiment he conducted with Harcourt at an international seminar, on the ability to reproduce random strings of letters and nonsense words approximating closely to various languages. There was no difference in ability to handle random strings, but a real difference in ability, favouring one's mother tongue, in reproducing nonsense in one's own language.˘ It is easy to place such nonsense words as MJOLKKOR, KLOOK, GERLANCH, OTIVANCHE, TRIANODE, FATTALONI, etc. As Bruner points out, when we learn a language we learn a coding system that goes beyond words. Now the coding system we usually think of when we talk about learning a language is usually spoken of as the 'grammar' of a language. And 'grammar' is concerned with the predictability of words and strings of words in their most likely sequence. There is a stronger probability of some words occurring next in a sequence than there is of others. There is no possibility of certain words following others in a particular language. We do not say 'Such a thing could not . . . some', or 'where', or 'food' or 'good' or 'judge', we could say 'be' or 'pertain' or 'happen'. Such word sequences are obviously greatly affected by meaning. Even so each word is on a scale of probability of occurrence from acceptable to wholly unacceptable and this applies to every word in turn. It is an example of what is known as the stochastic process which is any process governed by the laws of probability. In the case of the language process the expected probability of occurrence of any single element in sequence, from the point of view of the reader or listener, is governed by the immediate context and his previous personal experience of similar kinds of context.

Now, far from being the unsystematic, unpredictable collection of words handed down from a muddled and motley collection of etymological sources, spelling is just another example of this stochastic process. For in spelling we are concerned with letter sequences not word sequences. *Spelling is a kind of grammar for letter sequences that generates permissible combinations without regard to sound* (Gibson and Levin, 1975). As in word sequences (grammar) there is a scale of probability-range from letters that can occur in sequence to those that cannot occur, i.e. from highly probable to highly improbable even impossible letter sequences. We must remember of course that although this is a kind of grammar for letter sequences *within* a word, the spelling can be affected by grammatical and meaningful constraints, as in the case of homophones, where, for example, the spelling of 'mist' or 'missed' depends on the context. Indeed, Albrow (1972), in describing the English Writing System, sees many of its irregularities as ceasing to be irregular if we accept that there are different conventions in spelling for representing different grammatical and meaningful elements.

The coding system consists, then, of the most probable combination of letters in words, the groups of letters that tend to go together. The good speller has learnt the probable sequences of letters in words in his own language and these he has learned visually. But the young child, without much experience of the look of words, has a long way to go before he can unhesitatingly select the correct sequence from the various possible alternative letter sequences.

We hear words before we speak them. We speak them before we write them down. The sound of the word precedes the appearance by a very long way, and much visual experience of words is necessary before the individual can select the right one of the many possible alternatives for any English words and before the serial probabilities of letters are so fixed that he unfailingly selects the right one. It will be expected, then, that familiarity with serial probability will be derived mainly from reading experience, in other words, that ability to spell may well be 'caught' in the process. The role of incidental learning in spelling has consequently been one of the main preoccupations of research workers, and this must now be considered.

Caught or taught? The incidental/ systematic controversy

Before the turn of the century, when the teaching of spelling was standard practice in schools, there were rumblings about whether spelling needed to be taught at all.

The caught or taught debate has been thought by some to be simplistic, because, obviously, nobody catches any kind of skill without also being taught it. It would indeed be considered simplistic if 'caught' implied maturation, involving some kind of spelling acquisition device, and even then there would be outside influences at work. As we shall see, 'caught' means picked up in certain favourable circumstances in the context of concerned and perceiving adults. Nevertheless it is a debate which has incurred the attention of numerous research workers and vexed generations of teachers.

Was it not possible, then, that children would just 'catch' it as they learned to read and write? A classic article entitled 'The Futility of the Spelling Grind' (Rice, 1897) appeared, and this was followed up by, for example, Cornman (1902) criticising the systematic teaching of spelling and suggesting, with statistical evidence, that spelling could be approached through other activities such as written work and reading. The possibility of spelling being 'caught' rather than 'taught' was challenged soon after by Wallin (1910) with further statistical evidence in favour of the 'taught' rather than 'caught' school. So what came to be known as the incidental/systematic controversy had come to stay, simmering in America, but not boiling until the second quarter of the century with Grace Fernald, who in *Remedial Techniques in Basic School Subjects* (1943, p. 206) emphasised that the 'most satisfactory spelling vocabulary is that supplied by the child himself' in the course of his own expression. Kyte (1948) supported this view with reservations, advocating the withdrawal of good spellers from formal spelling lessons. Even these, he said, would need to be regularly tested, to ensure that they maintained their competence.

The role of incidental learning had become respectable. 'Incidental learning is indirect learning', wrote Hildreth (1956, p. 33), 'which takes place when the learner's attention is centred not on improving the skill in question, but on some other objective' and qualified this a moment later with, 'Teachers should not think of incidental learning and integrated teaching as excluding systematic well organized drill. Rather from the child's attempts to write will come evidence of his need for systematic word study.' So not only the spelling will be 'caught', but the need to learn to spell also. The comprehensive Scottish 'Studies in Spelling' (1961) took a firm line on the side of a systematised approach to the teaching of spelling: 'pupils following a systematic method make much greater progress and retain their learning better than those given no directions for learning to spell' (Patterson 1961, p. 85).

The 1970 research

The writer's own research through the 1960s showed where we stood at that time in the incidental/systematic controversy. By that time, with increasing preoccupation with class differences, educational opportunities and linguistic disadvantage, it might have been assumed, if it had been thought of at all, that good spelling was 'caught' in that nexus of linguistic advantage that is the heritage of the favoured child. From the investigation throughout a local education authority, and through the primary school years, it had indeed become clear that 'favoured' children, who had acquired good verbal ability, tend to learn to spell without much difficulty. But it was not quite as simple as that, and what contributed to their ease in learning to spell was both subtle and unexpected.

What became even clearer from the investigation was that children who did not catch spelling did learn to spell, provided that they were given good teaching. Good teaching implies a rational, consistent systematic approach to the teaching of the skill and through it all children can become 'good at spelling'!

How this can be brought about will be discussed throughout this book. First, however, we must consider what helps children to catch spelling.

What was it in the research undertaken by the writer that unearthed the practical measures set out, measures now being taken effectively by many teachers? From the research carried out, there emerged three main elements, three factors essential to learning to spell successfully:

1 Verbal ability.
2 Visual perception of word form.
3 Perceptuo-motor ability.

1 Verbal ability

This was the factor most predictive of spelling ability. It was seen to be so in the Swedish investigation into the structure of spelling ability (Ahlstrom 1964). It involved language enrichment and training, for example, familiarising children with the structure and use of words.

This was the verbal factor Townsend (1947) spotted when she showed the higher correlation between spelling and vocabulary than between spelling and reading comprehension, or spelling and tests of academic aptitude, and it is to be expected that word enthusiasts are able to spell well, whether their enthusiasm stems from etymology, trained eloquence or crossword puzzles. The Swedish analysis showed skill in reading and spelling to be related to each other, but some aspects of reading to be more closely related to spelling than others, particularly reading aloud. 'Reading aloud seems to be associated with skill in spelling, since in principle at least it is possible to read and spell words correctly without having any idea of their meaning.' (Ahlstrom 1964, p. 37). Reading aloud entails the auditory analysis which is essential to the spelling of words that are phonemically regular. It also associates the look of the word with the articulated and heard sound of the word. Articulation itself is helped and hence spelling, since

15

children with a very poor spoken language tend to be bad spellers.

It all stems from the attention given by the parent and teacher, not only talking with and being regulated by children and reading to and with children, but by their deliberately indicating structure and use of words to the children. And it is interest in reading that, throughout life, reflects verbal ability. Here the operative word is 'interest' for as we saw earlier, reading alone does not determine whether a child will be good at spelling. It is specialist interest that makes one look carefully at a particular word. The child who is reading to learn will read more slowly, more attentively, will focus on words relating to concepts that are important to him.

It will be recalled also that reading aloud is conducive to good spelling. This is because reading aloud not only paces the reader, enabling him to look at words more slowly, but because he is negotiating the syntax as he predicts, forces him to look carefully at the words he reads. The fact that we can read aloud without rehearsal, but with correct stress and intonation, depends upon our making a preliminary grammatical analysis. And it is in so doing that the child looks closely at words and it is this that provides the bonus in good spelling.

2 Visual perception of word form

The next most powerful predictor of spelling ability was visual perception of word form. This in the test situation showed children's ability to reproduce briefly exposed words, words of which they did not know the meaning but which contained common letter sequences. These they had to look at, by imaging and reconstituting the words. It is rather what happens in composing a sentence when a word needs to be written 'at the point of utterance'.

This reconstitution has to become automatic and to achieve this we must examine this process in detail. To be able to reconstitute a word seen fleetingly involves:

1 being able to 'read' the word;
2 being able to recall the 'read' word;
3 having recalled the first letter/string of letters, to reconstruct the rest, letter after letter or letter sequence after letter sequence;
4 being able to encode graphemically.

This, in fact, is equivalent to the factor in the Swedish analysis called *immediate memory for visual material*, and there is considerable supporting evidence of its importance. Now this is something which it has been found possible to train. We have seen that good spellers were distinguished by their immediate memory span for meaningful visual stimuli, and Gilbert and Gilbert (1942), who demonstrated the possibility of decreasing perceptual time while increasing proficiency in both immediate and delayed recall, advocated reducing time spent on learning to spell to an optimal level.

If nonsense approximations to English were aimed at, there would be two bonuses, in increasing the span of apprehension, and exercising serial probability at the same time.

Hartmann (1931), it will be remembered, showed that good spellers were distinguished by their immediate memory span for meaningful visual stimuli. In this study, visual perception of word form was strongly predictive of spelling attainment at nine and at eleven years, but was negatively associated with percentage progress (in other words with those who made most progress from a low initial level). This again suggests that the ability to fixate and then retain and reconstitute a word is something acquired by more favoured children in the early years, but that lack of this ability can be supplemented or compensated for by good teaching. For time spent on attention to word structure was a powerful predictor of actual progress in the teaching variable. In addition, children receiving no spelling teaching deteriorated rather than improved in rational attack in conformity with spelling precedent, an activity which clearly necessitates visual perception of word form.

What then is revealed in this factor that contributes to our knowledge of the nature of the spelling process?

1 Efficient visual perception of word form is acquired by favoured children (i.e., it is strongly associated with other linguistic abilities).
2 It can be supplemented or compensated for, when children are taught to pay attention to word structure.
3 Among favoured children, and this includes children taught to read by a rule-following procedure, it is a front-line strategy when habitual spelling breaks down. (This fact can be inferred from the study of generalising processes at nine and ten years.)
4 Efficient visual perception of word form is a necessary prerequisite to reconstitution of a long word briefly exposed.

These conclusions about the importance of the components of visual perception in spelling were confirmed in a particular exercise conducted in order to examine the role of serial probability in learning to spell.

Teachers usually accept that if spelling is a necessary skill, it is a skill which has to be learned. Yet when faced with the question of generalisation of letter sequence through knowledge of serial probability, they begin to talk about maturation and cognitive levels of development, forgetting that this generalisation is not on a conscious logical plane but at a mechanical, imaging, kinaesthetic level. In good spellers this is automatised, though in remedial spelling less favoured children have to be made aware of the mechanisms of generalisation before it becomes automatised.

Earlier in this chaper, mention was made of an analysis of children's spelling, at ten years, of the word 'saucer' (see Table 1). It is probable that many of these children had never written the word before. This then was a useful word to consider in connection with serial probability. How do children come to

TABLE 1   The spelling, by 967 ten year old children, of the word 'saucer'
(total number 988)*

Alternatives

sauser	67	seser		sarter	scoue	sosed
sorser	23	soer		sary	scour	sosar
suacer	23	sora		sascaue	scouse	sosiar
sacer	20	sorsa		sasger	scuace	sosre
sorcer	18	sos		sasere	scuarcer	sou
soser		sose	2	sasher	scuccer	sourcer
soucer	11	sosr		satard	scare	sourses
sucer		suar		saucere	scuser	sout
suser	10	sus		saucor	senrd	sowew
sawser	9	susar		saucing	serner	space
sarser		suse		saucher	sem	spanger
sarcer				saucter	ses	spcae
sacar	8	carser		saue	sesaur	spienace
sauce		causer		saues	sharser	sres
scaucer		chocer		saught	shasers	slous
souser	7	cor		saura	shose	suace
sauer	5	corroce		saurse	shower	suarser
sause		corser	1	saus	shure	suaser
caucer		curser		sauscer	sice	sucar
sawer		eswas		sausery	sinder	succer
socer		sacar		sausir	sined	sucase
sorer	4	sacca		sausue	slart	suce
surcer		saccar		sausur	sloy	sucger
surser		sacerer		savcr	smory	suecher
scauer		sacir		sawers	soc	sueer
saser		sacuere		sawur	socp	sucur
saurcer		sacuers		sayser	splorns	sud
saurser		saer		seacar	soolle	suger
scarcer	3	saeucng		scace	sooser	suier
suscer		sancer		searces	sooucer	sumser
suarcer		saose		scarsere	sor	suorser
sausar		sarce		scarser	sore	surage
cacer		sarear		scaser	sorcr	surce
sauccer		sare		scasur	sororr	surer
sarsar		saresir		scauser	sors	sureer
saursar		sari		scocer	sorsar	sursar
scar	2	sarig		scoors	sorscur	sursur
scare		saroer		scorceri	sorb	surts
scaser		sarry		scoser	sorur	susare
scorer		sarses		scoua	sorus	susas
sercer				scoucel	sosa	sues
						sye
						syer

Correct	462
Incorrect	505
*Omitted by	21

write the word 'saucer' correctly, never having learned to spell it, written it nor perhaps even read it?

It is useful to examine the alternatives offered by the children and the frequency with which they are offered. The most frequently presented alternative is 'sauser' (presented 67 times, i.e., 7 per cent), a very reasonable alternative. The vowel combinations are correct; only the internal consonant has been substituted. The next more frequent alternatives are 'suacer' and 'sorser', both offered 23 times. The word 'suacer' contains a vowel transposition, a visual error often made by children who do not look carefully at words. On the other hand 'sorser' could come about in several ways. It could derive from faulty auditory perception. The child hears the spoken word in a distorted way and reproduces this. Usually this is incorrect. Only once in the 967 children did faulty auditory perception produce some structural resemblance within a not only reasonable, but even poetically acceptable alternative when the phrase 'flowing shower' was offered in place of 'flying saucer'!

To write the word 'saucer' the child images and articulates the word sub-vocally. Then according to his visual and motor experience he writes swiftly and the word may or may not be correct.

It is not so much as Fernald (1943) said, a curve of mastery for each word, but a curve of visuo-motor experience of writing a particular letter sequence, which may or may not match the phonemes he has heard or articulated. The more often he associates the articulated and heard sound (in relation to sounds immediately succeeding and preceding it) *together with the written sequence* the greater the probability of his repeating this sequence in relation to the preceding and succeeding letter sequences. This is what is meant by generalisation of letter sequences. But it must occur at the same time as writing it.

It is significant in this context, that time spent by teachers on attention to word structure was seen to determine actual progress in spelling, but children receiving no teaching, and children blindly pursuing a printed word list with no instructions about how to learn the words, deteriorated in their ability to write words that conformed to precedent in English. In other words, children who were not taught to look carefully at the internal structure of words did not make 'good' errors. This ability to write 'good' errors, that is, errors which are very nearly right and which could happen, like writing 'verry' for 'very' demonstrates an ability to generalise from knowing what letter sequences look like. Thus, from knowing a sequence like 'cou' in 'count', the child can generalise to 'courage' and 'cousin' and 'court'.

As Bradley (1981) showed, the actual writing of the spelling patterns establishes them within even difficult and irregular words.

3 Perceptuo-motor ability

So we come to writing, and the third most predictive factor was the one termed *carefulness*, evinced in the quality of handwriting, the relevant criteria being well-formed, legible and barely legible handwriting. Now this might well suggest that children who are able to spell well at nine are, as they write carefully, deliberately and intelligently, assessing the possible alternative strategies necessary to spelling as they write. But carefulness in writing is significantly correlated with speed of handwriting, and both these factors correlate significantly with good spelling. So these children who write carefully tend to write more swiftly. That casual and slow handwriting are correlated is of interest since there is here implied an uncertainty about letter formation and a time-consuming uncertainty about letter sequence as well as letter formation. It is worth noting that slow speed of handwriting is the most important element in percentage progress (which highlights those children who begin at a very low attainment level but make most progress). It is more important than poor verbal intelligence or poor visual perception of word form. Speed of writing is clearly basic to spelling progress.

It is not possible to plumb the origin of this slowness. Speed of writing is correlated with verbal intelligence. But speed of writing is an aspect of a motor skill much more akin to walking or riding a bicycle than spelling is. Such skills are acquired through successive approximations to the most economic and effective movement, and learned through identification, imitation and practice. This, if anything, would seem to be an area within the teaching orbit. Writing, whether acquired through copying, or preferably finger-tracing a written reproduction (Fernald 1943), would seem to be directly a contributory sub-skill of spelling, and indirectly of creative writing, that it is disastrous to neglect.

These, then, are the kind of elements which make spelling a skill, which constitute the kind of strategies undertaken when habitual spelling breaks down. These are the elements which must be taught if spelling is indeed to become a habit, so that the individual can attend to the content of what he is writing.

A word must be said about vocalising while we write. There is uncertainty amongst research workers about the value and function of vocalising as we spell. There is no question that that is what we do, albeit sub-vocally. Hotopf (1980, p. 296), showing that the planning of speech and writing is in clauses, not bits such as phrases, writes 'it is indeed a common experience that we occasionally mutter to ourselves, or are aware of sub-vocal formulations ahead in our writing.'

Ways have been suggested of actually interfering with articulation or vocalisation in the cause of reading and spelling, the best known example of this being Luria's tongue-tying experiment, which not surprisingly inhibited the children's spelling!

If concurrent vocalisation does impair spelling, in that it is thought to affect phonological analysis, this is because the child's spelling is arising from vocalisation which does not occur at the same time. In writing the word 'friend', he first mutters 'fre' and it is inevitably incorrect. This is why it is so important that the spelling should be 'at his fingertips', a motor sequence as he writes. This, after all, is what happens when we write our name, however unusual and irregular it

22

may be. Such writing seems to be coded specifically for written output, independently of the speech route (Luria 1970, p. 222).

Though spelling is 'caught' by some, there are very strong reasons why it should be caught by all in the cause of communication, courtesy and habits of care. Though a worthwhile status symbol, it is in the freedom it gives one to express precisely that it is most valuable. It is an achievable skill in that we are simply dealing with a word. We become familiar with this serial probability through word usage and looking carefully at words and writing them, often muttering them as we write. This, then, is what the spelling skill is like. How then can it be caught?

2

How is it caught?

The linguistically favoured child seems to learn to spell as he learns the performance of other linguistic skills. He, as it were, catches the ability, for 'To him that hath shall be given'. Such children seem to catch spelling as easily as they catch singing.

These are favoured children, who indeed have good verbal intelligence, who have enjoyed their mother's care and concern in the pre-school years. But some mothers have done something else as well as just talking and reading to their children. Such a mother has, while reading stories, while shopping, while watching television, etc. not only pointed out words to her child, but lightly and incidentally, indicated the internal structure of the words the two of them come up against. Such behaviour is as 'natural' to the caring mother as her early 'expansion' of two-word utterances when her child was beginning to talk.

In the writer's research (1970) it was clear that though the children who had 'caught' spelling tended to be those who had acquired high verbal intelligence, the most important attribute they possessed was 'good visual perception of word forms' with all that implies. Quite simply, these children had not merely been given opportunities to read and be read to, but the internal structure of words had been pointed out to them, not only in books, but in the world of words surrounding them, their names, the names of foods and sweets, road signs or street names. 'That bit's like a bit in your name,' says his mother to Martin as he eats his Smarties or his Mars bar and she is helping him to catch spelling very nicely.

The child who said, 'She's in me because she's Anna and I'm Joanna' had learned to look with interest at the internal structure of words. These children are indeed 'catching' spelling. We can say that these children have become sensitised to the coding system of our orthography.

An example of a young pre-school child noticing the internal structure of words is four-year-old Jonathan. One day he was reading to himself and came to 'There is Peter'. He proceeded to cover over the 'T' and read 'Here is Peter'. He then covered over the 'e' at the end of 'here' and read 'Her is Peter' and remarked 'That's silly!' Needless to say he became a very good speller!

It is this kind of empirical and anecdotal evidence that makes us look very closely at the role of incidental learning in spelling, that is, at the early catching of the sub-skills of spelling.

It is the interested parent who initiates looking with interest at words. It is the interested and perceptive parent who discusses with the pre-school child the experiences of the day, reviewing these serially: 'First we went to Granny's, then we went to the supermarket.' This is the way into extending the child's imaging, another useful contribution to his catching of spelling.

And while developing the child's imagery, the parent is increasing his serial span of apprehension, both very important attributes of the child who is catching spelling.

Is it caught through reading?

It might be expected that the children who catch spelling are those who have already learned to read. Teachers reassure worried parents by telling them, 'Don't worry, his spelling will improve when he reads more!' This is one of the many myths that surround the spelling skill. He will not, in fact, just 'catch' spelling by reading. There are, as we all know, many highly intelligent, well-read and even literary people who are very poor spellers. These are frequently people who read at a very fast rate, who learned to read very quickly, often even before they went to school, at their mother's knee as she read them stories, while they followed the print as she read. They do not look, nor rarely, if ever, did they need to, at individual words, and this is the reason why they are frequently, but not necessarily, poor spellers.

In 1941 Nisbet pointed out that children are likely to 'catch' only one new word out of every twenty-five they read. With older people who are unsophisticated readers, this may also be true, but with serious, slower more focussed readers such as students, the gain in spelling ability from mere reading could be expected to be greater, particularly in more technical words that may be new to the student, who might pick up the spelling from the significant etymology of the word. As long ago as 1935, Gilbert found that college students' spelling certainly improved as they read, the extent of the improvements depending on the type of reading and the reader's purpose. Words that had been recently brought to their attention were 'caught' more effectively than words encountered more remotely, and good spellers learned more words than poor spellers. As Bryant and Bradley (1983) show, children read and spell in different ways. They neglect particular strategies when they read, but take them up when they spell and vice versa. Groff (1984) too, emphasises this difference, in comparing the word familiarity assumed in reading, with success in learning to spell. From the evidence relating to the catching of spelling through reading, it looks as if:

(a) Children are likely to learn how to spell (catch) only about 4 per cent of the words read (Nisbet 1941).
(b) College students' spelling improves by reading, particularly of words brought to their attention. Better spellers learn more new words through reading than poor spellers (Gilbert 1935).
(c) The casual experience of words in reading lessons is, in the case of young and backward children, insufficient for recording permanent impressions (Schonell 1942).

(d) Not all children need formal spelling lessons, though the competence of any such children in spelling must be tested regularly (Kyte 1948).

(e) 'Catching' words incidentally seems to occur when children's attention is centred on some object other than improving the skill itself (Hildreth 1956).

Why then is spelling so completely different from reading? The difference has been characterised as being 'analogous to that between recognition and recall' (Gibson and Levin 1975, p. 335), but reading is far more than mere recognition though spelling is indeed dependent on recall.

First, reading skill is flexible. Considerable variation is possible in performance, depending on the purpose for which one is reading, but in spelling, variation is not acceptable. Spelling does not vary according to the occasion, except in so far as shorthand takes place of longhand when a secretary receives dictation.

Second, reading is a skill that allows successive approximation to the word being read before commitment, while spelling has a permanence about it. Once it is written it is written. (Unless it is erased.)

Third, the most important difference between reading and spelling is the nature of the skill itself. Reading skills depend on the child's ability to tap his various linguistic resources, syntactic and semantic, in order to supplement what is presented on the printed page. Spelling is not as complex a skill as reading. It is, as we have seen, a single skill which is ultimately a motor habit of the hand.

Fourth, reading is predictive not reactive. The reader looks ahead and does not necessarily focus on a particular word. It is the relationship of words one with another that informs the reader. In spelling it is the relationship of *letters* and sequences of letters *within* the word. It is only rarely, as in the case of homophones, that the meaning affects the spelling.

Does poor hearing prevent the catching of spelling?

It might be expected that children with poor hearing might be handicapped in spelling. But this does not seem to be so. Comparing the spelling of deaf children with normal children of the same reading ability, the deaf children were found to be superior by three or four years (Gates and Chase 1926). Templin, too, in 1954 found that both deaf and hard of hearing children made substantially fewer errors than hearing children in theme writing and these early observations have been supported by repeated studies, quoted by Dodd (1980).

It is probable that these children relied almost exclusively on the visual pattern of word structure as they wrote, since by definition they were unable to differentiate small auditory differences and English spelling as has been demonstrated at length, demands awareness of visual rather than auditory patterns. In other words, deaf children seem to prefer graphemic codes in spelling.

Is it caught through listening?

A second possibility might be that it is partly picked up by listening. But this is obviously a very implausible suggestion. Only in the case of words that have no possible alternatives, within our coding system is listening of service to correct spelling. With all other words, listening offers limited clues. Even in a word such as 'where' (only the pedantic sound the h) we are given no auditory clue. So many poor spellers confuse it with 'wear' or even the shorter 'were', or confuse 'off' and 'of', in spite of the difference in sound. Homophones, which are words that sound the same but are spelled differently, depend upon grammar and meaning if they are to be spelled correctly. If the writer connects the look of the word with its meaning and not with its sound, confusions such as 'there' for 'their' would not occur. When the poor speller is confronted by a multi-syllabic word, he may well produce an auditory image of the word, and separate it into syllables which can be written out one at a time, even though many of these syllables present the possibility of several alternative spellings.

A recurring item in radio and TV panel games is the request for a long word to be spelled, and it is possible to identify the victims' methods of attack, in other words whether they were relying on visual or auditory memory. The visualisers read off the word quickly, and usually correctly. Those who rely on auditory memory, spell syllabically, and the listener is aware of the point of uncertainty – 'sacrilegious' would be spelt 'sacril', and then uncertainly, 'lig' or 'leg'? Unsupported by other imagery, this is a precarious means to spelling.

Attending to the sound of the word can really only be helpful where a single letter corresponds with a phoneme, like 'a' in 'bat' or 'can', and even then there will be confusion when we come to words like 'as', 'was' and 'ask'. But it is in that small proportion of grapho-phonemically irregular words and that bigger proportion of words that, though regular, have some reasonable alternative, that auditory attention is no use. And there is no sense in relying on a system that breaks down just when one needs it most. Indeed in reading, 'an over emphasis on phonics in teaching reading is apt to produce some poor spellers, especially if one-to-one letter sound correspondence is emphasised' (Gibson and Levin 1975, p. 335), for 'traditional phonics', we read (Williamson and Wooden 1980, p. 31), 'tends to generate a morass of confusion because the focus of its principles and generalisations are only on phoneme-grapheme correspondences.'

Does poor sight prevent the catching of spelling?

In the light of emphasis placed throughout this book on the importance of looking, it might be expected that children with poor sight might be handicapped in spelling. Apart from the inevitable handicaps and their repercussions on spelling experienced by the partially sighted, children who have to wear glasses and yet are within the range of normality, spell as well as those who do not. It is not acuity of vision that distinguishes the good spellers from the bad (Russell 1937).

It is possible that if the visual field is limited for some reason, the child, like a horse in blinkers, sees only a small area at a time. This could explain the smaller visual memory span often found in poor spellers (Spache 1940). It does not look as if impaired visual acuity which makes a child unable to discriminate visually between letters, is a cause of inability to spell as much as it is an earlier cause of inability to read. Even in reading, isolated sensory deficiencies have hardly ever been shown to be insurmountable handicaps (Fendrick 1935).

With normal children spelling ability is not so much affected by slight peripheral disabilities as by central difficulties (Hartmann 1931). In other words it is not the eyes and the ears but what goes on behind them that really affects spelling; the perceptual rather than the sensory mechanisms are decisive.

It is important at the outset to distinguish between neural impairment which is very readily confused with sensory disability. The child's ears and eyes may be efficient but the child still cannot hear or see. What looks like perceptual disability may of course be habitual lack of attention, for severe neural impairment of the kind that would inevitably affect reading and spelling is rare.

There seems to be, however, one aspect of the perceptual process that really does affect spelling. Hartmann (1931) spoke of it as a particular 'form of looking', which was quite distinct from any specific sensory ability or facility in integrating such sensory abilities.

Let us consider what is meant by this particular 'form of looking'. Although the small span of visual apprehension found in poor spellers can be associated with a visual field limited optically, in the retina itself, it is what goes on when a child reproduces a word from a flash card that is interesting in this connection. Good spellers perceive total configurations or, one might say, see the word as a whole more easily than poor spellers (Hartmann 1931). Now we work on the assumption that perceptual disabilities can be compensated for in training, and we know that the more familiar words are, the more likely we are to see them as a whole (Howes and Solomon 1951). So this may well be a means of training this perception of wholes, by teaching the child to spell words already familiar to him. It is a strong justification for the infant school practice of 'catching words' and of making a start at learning the word as a whole when written in his personal dictionary by the teacher, and not blindly copying.

The need to look at words as wholes has been repeatedly observed. As early as 1923, Hilderbrandt suggested that, in learning to spell, it was unwise to lay too much stress on phonic elements, as these might well obstruct the view of the word as a sequence of significant parts or as a whole. Again in 1936, Higley and Higley recommended that, in learning to spell a word, a child should, in the first instance, just look at the word without saying, spelling or writing it, as these intrusions might confuse his learning.

'Looking at a word as a whole' is a vague term which has been heavily and justifiably criticised by supporters of phonic reading schemes (e.g. Diack 1960). What this phrase means, in terms of spelling needs, is that the word must be reproducible when exposed for a short time on a tachistoscope or a flash card. For this the word must be either familiar (in terms of reading experiences) or short enough to be within the individual's span of apprehension for unconnected elements. The more familiar the word, the longer it can be. Presumably a word that is familiar to a child in the process of his reading, when exposed on a flash card, is not merely reproduced in a memory image, but recognised as in reading and then in recall *built up into its component parts*. The word is not recalled but remade in the light of the child's reading experience with this particular word. It might have been thought that this would not help in dealing with unfamiliar words; hence the preoccupation of teachers with syllabification, with marking hard spots, etc. But reproducing the word correctly, when it is both new and long, depends on first being able to read it, and then in the light of experience with groups of letters that go together (the old 'sequential probability'), being able to reconstruct the word in plausible forms.

If, on the other hand, we do not limit the time of exposure of a word, by tachistoscope or flash card, but give the child time to study a word he is to spell, his eyes move about the word, lighting on different parts for varying lengths of time and going back over parts again. From looking at such eye-movements it is known that good spellers make fewer and shorter fixations than poor spellers, see more of the word at a time, and make fewer regressive movements. Younger and less mature children are also less efficient in eye-movements than older children (Gilbert and Gilbert 1942).

Inefficiency of eye-movements is a perceptual habit which is not a cause of but a concomitant of poor spelling. Gilbert and Gilbert (1942) put the cause of this in poor study habits, over-emphasis and overstudy, thoroughness rather than efficiency. Gilbert's study techniques to overcome this will be described in a later chapter.

Is it caught through looking?

If looking alone were enough to make us into good spellers, and if indeed the reader looked at each word, reading would be the answer, and we have shown this only to be the case with older people who had a mental set towards their particular subject or interest, and in the case of those who are good spellers already, for whom just to look was often enough to improve their spelling ability even further. Just looking does not seem to be enough. Spelling ability comes no more from being able to see than being able to hear. Hartmann (1931) showed that spelling ability was not affected by how far or how well one could see, yet there was one special aspect of seeing that was closely related to spelling, one special reaction that affected spelling.

He showed that if meaningful words were exposed on a tachistoscope, or more simply on flash cards of the kind used in school, more were taken in as wholes by good spellers than by poor spellers. This is possibly because good spellers exercise their imagery. Having perceived a word pattern or configuration, they hold on to this and, while holding on to it, examine it, observing the characteristics of this particular word-form. And training in visual imagery can improve spelling. It has been shown that spelling is improved by as little as two weeks' training in visual imagery, the effects showing a year later when imagery-trained groups scored significantly higher on spelling tests than untrained groups (Radaker 1963). This training in visual imagery is an example of how one can direct the attention of the individual to visual characteristics, to the appearance of the word, and this seems to be a very efficient way of exploiting our preferred sense – it is the way into how spelling is 'caught'.

Though training in imagery seems to help in learning to spell, it is probably not merely the imaging alone, but instead, as Sloboda (1980) argues, 'Good spellers achieve their results, not by virtue of particular skills, but by virtue of their memory for the way individual words are spelled' and, it might be added, by generalisation from the structures within these individual words to other new and unknown words for, to quote Frith (1980), 'visual factors in spelling have nothing to do with visual appearance but concern letter-by-letter structure' – what we call letter patterns, or letter strings, in the context of serial probability.

Would spelling be caught more easily by a simplified spelling system?

It might be thought that if the spelling system were to be simplified, we might experience short-term advantages in learning to spell. For we should write entirely from the sound, which, as we shall see, is what misguided teachers of our present spelling system often try to do with sad results.

It might be thought that the short-term advantages in a simplified spelling system might have other advantages, particularly in reading. This was indeed the case for the development of i.t.a., the Initial Teaching Alphabet, in the 1950s. There were indeed short-term advantages in that, both in swift and early decoding ability and in free writing using this simplified alphabet, and contrary to the expectation of most teachers, the spelling of children taught by i.t.a. was overall no worse than that of children taught to read in traditional orthography. That was because teachers of i.t.a. just had to teach spelling, and on the whole they did this systematically and efficiently.

The difficulty with any simplified spelling system is that it would, once children had learned to decode it, also reduce our reading efficiency. 'How cumbersome', wrote Gimson (1968, p. 339) 'it would be if we were to write with phonetic accuracy'; it would 'provide us with a great deal more information than we need for the visual comprehension of our own language . . . our present imperfect writing system allows speed of reading at least double that of speech.' Carol Chomsky suggests that the phonetic transcription of words in writing may be a positive distraction when one considers that 'the conventional spelling system leads the reader directly to the meaning-bearing items'. If, for example, we are reading the word 'telegraphically' we home in to the informative bits 'tele . . gr . ph . .' and, because we are anticipating, and have made a preliminary grammatical foray into the sentence as we read, we have no trouble in reading the word correctly without looking in detail at the whole word. As Frith (1980, p. 515) points out, the minimal cues used for word recognition that result in highly efficient reading provide little help for spelling. 'There is', she writes, 'a cost in the elegant economy and speed of reading by partial cues, namely, poor spelling.' Another different point about writing exactly as we speak, that is phonetically, is that personal accents would be written down as the sound and communication between people from different parts of the country or world would be made more difficult. For spelling written down irons out accents. As Trudgill (1983, p. 60) wrily observes, 'English spelling is probably sufficiently distant from pronunciation not to favour one accent over another; all speakers are at an equal disadvantage.' And so they are as long as they rely for their spelling on pronunciation!

Again our body of literature and all our texts are printed in a form that could not easily be reprinted in simplified spelling. Change-over from the 'old money' to 'metric' would be nothing to the problems of a universal change-over to a simplified spelling system. As Brazil (1982, p. 155) optimistically observes, 'It is worth noting a healthy trend towards trying to understand our orthographic system, instead of trying to reform it!'

It is clear, then, that to achieve the 'machine-like movements in spelling', we cannot rely on the practice of reading alone to teach us how to spell. We cannot rely on the sound, either heard or imaged, since the alternative spelling possibilities for many syllables make this a very chancy system. Yet looking by itself without training in attention to word forms or training in imagery is not enough. Is the answer then, that we should rely on a multi-sensory approach involving visual, auditory, kinaesthetic and articulatory inroads? Or should we rely on looking, through careful training in the sphere of vision, for example, in attention, in imagery, and in the learning of probable word patterns and sequences? These two alternatives suggest two main and rational ways of teaching spelling. The first is by a sensory amalgam such as Fernald used. She offered a system that would bridge individual differences of sensory preference or habit of imagery. By a system of reinforcement, where finger-tracing concurs with all the other sensory inroads, the child cannot help acquiring the pattern of the words he is learning. He is drilling himself and he is over-learning each word.

This is a safe and certain way, and, though time-consuming, is often the only way for children with severe spelling difficulties. The second is by directing the attention of the individual to the particular characteristics of the word-form and consolidating these in writing. They are alternatives to the haphazard, ad hoc learning that goes on when children are given lists to learn without being given psychologically sound and tried strategies with which to learn them.

It emerged from the investigations quoted above that those children who have not 'caught' spelling do learn to spell if they are given good teaching. This implies a willingness on the part of the teacher to point out the internal structure of words. The good teacher is in fact training visual perception of word-forms, an ability that the favoured child acquired early in his school life. What the teacher is in fact doing is teaching the catching of spelling, and it is with how she does this that the next chapter is concerned.

3

Teaching the catching of spelling for those who have not already caught it

Directing attention

In order to teach those children who have *not* caught the skill, it is important for the teacher to know what contributed to the success of those who *have*.

Spelling is not, as we have seen, 'caught' just through reading. It is certainly not through listening, since the English spelling system can have more than one spelling for any one sound, e.g. cup, done, does, blood, tough, and more than one sound for any one spelling, e.g. does, goes, canoe. It is almost certainly 'caught' in the early years through looking, but, as we have seen, through looking in a specially intent way. It is 'caught' through the child's developing forms of imagery and serial reconstructions and, as a consequence of this, becoming accustomed to the probability of letter sequences occurring. The children who have 'caught' spelling are familiar with these sequences in the world around them. They are, as we have said, sensitised to the coding of English and this is in a benign social context where parents and teachers are reviewing, commenting on and predicting events in the child's day, e.g. shared activities which are regulated by the child in speech and in writing.

The task of the teacher is, therefore, to put those children who have not 'caught' the skill into the way of looking with intent, and collecting a bank of letter sequences (or 'letter strings' or as the children call them 'letter patterns') from which they can generalise, to the new words they need to write. She also teaches well-formed handwriting and uses opportunities (not wasting them) to pursue joint activities, conversations and correspondences with individual children as well as with groups.

Attention and perception

On every hand we are beset with stimuli, sights, sounds, smells, the feel of things, tastes, etc., and from all these competing attractions we select for our attention only one bit of input. We only perceive that bit to which we attend and, of course, we tend to remember what we have perceived. But it is the first element of all this that is important, the selection of what to perceive. This is where the caring and concerned mother or teacher takes over when she actively and deliberately *points out* what seems to be important in the environment for the child to select and attend to. The 'environment' would be a pale and bland world without the perceiving mind of the adult. 'Oh, look at this furry caterpillar!' 'Can you see the girl with the skipping rope?' 'Listen, I can hear a cuckoo, can you?'

We know, only too well, something pointed out very strikingly by Wells (1981) when he shows that it is the child's own directing and initiating that engenders more and better conversation. This does not occur except within a warm and inviting parent/child or teacher/child relationship and it certainly stems in the very beginning from the time the mother 'points out' things in the world around to the very small baby in his pram and when she demands responsive cooing by fixating him with eye-to-eye contact, talking to him and then *waiting* for seconds at a time till he responds. As the baby learns what kinds of things bring about these kinds of responses, he is learning to behave intentionally (McShane 1980).

This is all the beginning of what is usually called 'directing attention'. It is teaching the child to select from incoming stimuli, to attend to and perceive those things that the parent or teacher deems to be important.

It is this directing of attention which is responsible for the 'looking in a very special way' that was discussed in the last chapter, and young children mainly look with intent at what is pointed out to them (as something to select and perceive), unless the stimulus is of high intensity or repetition like a bright light or repeated sound or series of the same picture or of something completely new within a familiar background environment. In the kind of looking with intent that we are talking about in the early years, it is looking with intent to pick out the interesting 'letter patterns' or 'letter strings' that are 'like my name' or like the name of a sweet or detergent, or other products that appear within the child's vicinity.

Now we do not 'look with intent' unless we have a reason for doing so. In the case of spelling this is to reproduce a word. Hence, this involves an intention on the part of the mother and/or teacher that the child should look closely at the name before writing it. To show an intention, it is necessary to state it for only in that way can the meaning of the intention be made clear to the child. At a very early age, the child can be reinforced in his intention to write his name by the mother or teacher pointing out the interesting features and expecting him to be able to reproduce this without copying.

The teacher lets the children give out named books and boxes, so that the children become familiar with Christian names that are characteristic of the spelling patterns of their own language structure. Children, too, are constantly requesting words to be put in their finger-tracing file or their personal dictionary, and here they are learning the possibilities of spelling patterns as the teacher points out interesting features within the words they ask for. More systematic observation of word-structure is important, however.

It would seem evident that this early pointing out of letter patterns causes children to 'catch' spelling. Further evidence is in the number of intelligent and even literary adults who are poor spellers who almost universally report that they learned to read early in life, often 'at their mother's knee'. Their poor spelling stems from their just *not* having needed to look closely at words as they read. They happily skipped along as they read with their mother, anticipating rather than reacting to the print. This, in school, is what used to be called learning to read by 'Look and Say', and as Dean (1968) stated, learning to read by 'look and say', is an approach unlikely to promote close examination of words. It is what Frith (1980) calls 'eye-to-print-to-meaning' rather than 'ear-to-print-to-sound-to-meaning' strategies, which is what is usually termed a 'phonic' or 'decoding' approach to reading. These intelligent and literary adults also report that they read very fast, so as adults they still do not look at the internal structure of words.

Parents' knowledge of the spelling system

If the parent or teacher is to be in a position to point out likenesses within words, she must herself be aware of these. The difficulty is that though she knows how to spell, that is to say she has a model of the spelling process, which some call a phonic map and some a mental lexicon, to refer to, she may not know what that model or map or mental lexicon looks like. She may learn what it is like by playing games like Scrabble or doing crosswords or just by being interested in word structure. This pointing out of letter patterns to children, however, does imply that she is aware of these. Further, the fact that she is aware of them and interested in them will motivate her to direct her child's attention to them.

In the writer's research, it was interesting to note that of the children who neither catch nor learn spelling very early, those who are favourably placed in family order, i.e. the oldest or the youngest, do in fact tend to progress well, since they are inevitably more accustomed to variable, exploratory and mutually satisfying talk, reading, as well as attending to words, than do children in the middle of a family.

A visual skill? How do we know?

Finally, if we need to be convinced about the fact that spelling is a visual skill, we only have to look at ourselves as adults. When we are uncertain about how to spell a word we *write it down to see if it looks right*. In other words, we check visually and, because we can read, because we have looked again and again at letter sequences in English, we see at once if the word is spelled correctly. We are completely secure when we see that a word *looks right*. Figure 1 shows some examples of adult's and children's writing of words which they were not sure how to spell. They tried out the word repeatedly before being satisfied.

After a careful exploration of the common-sense belief that adults know a spelling is correct if it 'looks right', whatever the prior basis for their knowing, Tenney (1980, p. 229) concludes, 'Do go and get a pencil the next time you find yourself writing with a finger in the air!'

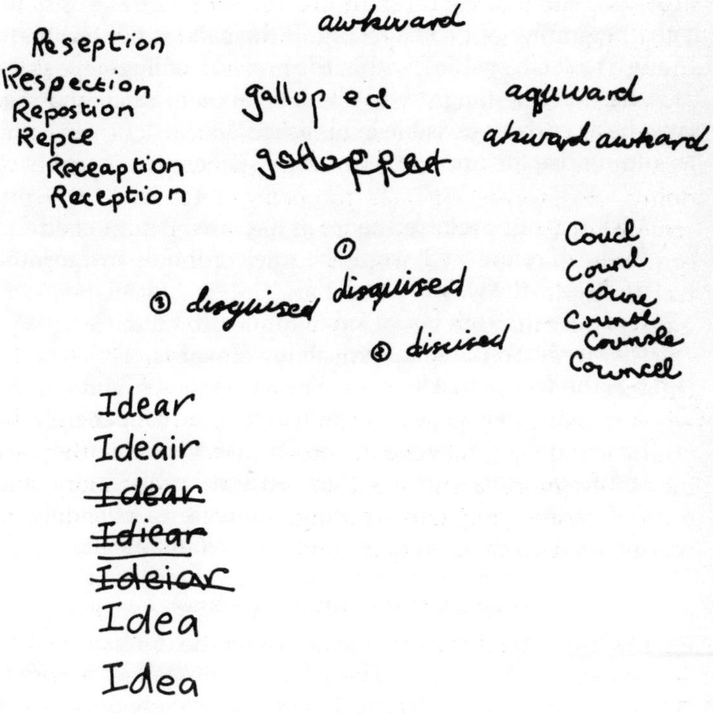

Figure 1

41

How then can we *teach* to all children what some have *caught* in the way of attending to learning and generalising from letter sequences?

Looking with intent

As we saw in Chapter 2, a child's own name is particularly important. It is the one thing the teacher cannot remove from him when he goes to school. Yet she ignores it when she gives him a cloakroom peg marked with a duck or a boat or a ball! This is a lost opportunity. By labelling the peg with a name, Mark, Martin or Mary, the four-year-old is soon able to distinguish his peg and his name. He is able to do this because he has to look. All this is in a real, day-to-day and not a contrived situation, and looking carefully at word structure at this stage is the beginning of good spelling. If the child is not fortunate enough to catch spelling within the network of linguistic skills then he must be taught what he has failed to catch and this must be as early as possible in his school life.

To summarise the importance of the visual mode:

1 Vision is our preferred sense as humans. If dogs need a frame of reference it would be smell. For humans, to look and see is the way of checking.
2 It is only through visual familiarity with written language that we learn the serial probability of words.
3 It is the words that look alike however they sound which, connected in groups according to their visual pattern, form meaningful connections. The use of mnemonics, i.e. the association with some learned and familiar connection, will reduce the amount to be learned and increase spelling ability as surely as 'group-labelling' has been seen to increase the span of apprehension.
4 Visual learning provides a check. We learn to spell a word. We look to see if it is correct. If it does not 'look right' we learn and check again. This is active self-testing, a most useful ally in every learning situation (Woodworth and Schlosberg 1955).

No other perceptual avenue provides such a
mechanism of verification as 'seeing with your own eyes'.

We do not learn anything and we certainly do not remember
what we have learned, unless we have actively attended to
what we are learning. It is unlikely that the young child will
attend to words unless an adult has specifically *drawn his
attention* to them and to their structure. The mother who has
pointed out to Ja*son* that he is her *son*, that *Mar*tin likes S*mar*ties
and that T*imothy* collects *moth*s is drawing attention to word
structure, and, as we have seen, it is this aspect of word play
that is much ignored. Such attending to words is of course
incidental. It is just having fun with words, which depends on
the mother's or teacher's knowing what the spelling system is
like. This is more than just being able to spell. A teacher must, if
she is to be able to direct children's attention to hard spots
within words, know words that 'look like' the word with
which the child is having trouble. She must be able to connect
such words at will, for example, for*war*d into *war*, compe*tent* at
pitching a *tent*, etc. and, having connected them, she must
point them out to him. Once having been noticed, the 'hard
spot' is no longer 'hard'.

What we are talking about here is generalisation to other
words which have the same internal structure. On the whole
children do not generalise unless they have been taught to
perceive likenesses within words. They must be told by the
teacher explicitly:

'These words look the same.' e.g. 'horse' and 'worse'.
'Look for the letter string that is the same.'
'What is that word like?'

This is the case for the 'Word Bank' produced by the writer in
collaboration with Cripps (1978). In this 'Word Bank' they are
told to *look* carefully at a word and particularly at the highlighted letter-string which is likely to be the 'hard spot' and
then look at this in the other words in the Bank. These they will
not actually learn by writing, but by relating letter strings.

They will acquire the secret of spelling by generalisation rather than by the tedious method of learning rules. For as is shown in the next chapter, rule-learning and generalisation from rules rather than from letter strings depends upon a developmental level of mental operation that is beyond many children.

If a child wants to write at all, he wants to write so that what he writes can be read. The content is important but he must be able to spell adequately enough for other people to be able to read what he has written. So he must have access to the correct spelling of the words he wants to use. Many of these will be in the Word Bank. Those that are not he must learn to ask for. The parent or teacher will write them for him, and he must learn not to copy, but to close the book before writing the word. There is a calculable chance that he will remember the word incorrectly, but it is the technique of learning that matters, not the particular word he wants. Moreover, this is the building up of a bank of words which will form the basis for his own spelling list, personal and important to him. From this he will acquire a repertoire of words which he can spell from his own vocabulary and in his own idiom.

The importance of associative learning techniques in the learning of unknown words

Why, when we are spelling, do we have problems at any 'hard spot'? No doubt, it is because we have not attended closely enough to that particular difficulty and often the only way we can remember it is either by seeing it as a word within a word, for example, 'ache' in 'teacher', 'hat' in 'what', or by generalising from a known letter string, for example, 'gar' in 'sugar and garden', 'augh' in 'laughter and daughter'. In other words, competent spellers who know what the spelling system is like automatically associate unknown words with known words.

Letter strings

The chance of deliberate directing of attention by the mother to letter strings in names is only the beginning and needs to be developed systematically by the teacher. This is where the production of word banks is so valuable. These are merely collections of words in the form of a book or a box, either for a child for himself or for the class as a whole, or as a set of wall pockets. Each page of the book or section of the box or wall pocket is devoted to one letter string. As the children meet words containing the letter string on the outside, they write the word on the appropriate page, or write it on a card and put it in a section of the box or in the wall pocket. The children collect and store in these the words they want to use in their writing, with the result that eventually a bank of words is created, that is, categorised according to the letter strings it contains. This is a useful resource for the whole class, since the words are those some of the rest of the class will want to write, since they are in the idiom of the group, For example, one page or box or pocket will be labelled 'wor' and contain words like 'worn, work, sword, worm'. Another will be labelled 'cou' and contain 'count, cousin, could, cough, country, couple'. In whatever form these are stored, it is crucial that when the children want to use them in the course of their free writing, they must do so without copying, which is why it is useful to have the words put away in the sections of the book or of the box or in the wall pocket and not on display on the wall.

It must be remembered that these are grouped according to the look of the words, not as phonics for reading lists. In other words, for spelling one must emphasise the importance of grouping together words which look the same irrespective of their sound.

Words within words

When competent spellers want to write 'conscience' they write it without thinking since they already know 'con' and 'science'. It flows from the end of the pen. It would seem reasonable then to point out deliberately to children the relationship between a known word and an unknown word. Then they can learn to write 'shoulder' because they know 'should', or 'heard' because they know 'ear' and 'hear'. They can be taught to look for words within the sequence of known words – e.g. in 'Liverpool' is 'live', 'liver', 'pool'; in 'Belfast' is 'fast', 'as' and 'elf' – and their own names are highly productive of words within words.

It must be made very clear to teachers and parents that we are not talking here about the game 'How many words can you make out of the word "Liverpool"?' i.e. irrespective of letters in sequence. Such games as this, and jumbled words and anagrams, are all very well for the good speller, but they are DISASTROUS for the poor speller or the young child.

To produce a word, irrespective of letter sequence, presented *out of* the word 'Liverpool' demands that a child thinks of a word, probably, by its first letter, e.g. 'L' and then has to *work out* how to spell 'love', or 'p' and then has to work out how to spell 'prove', or 'r' and then has to work out how to spell 'rope'. From 'Belfast', the child thinks of a word such as 'stable' but he has no help at all in how to spell it and might easily offer 'stable' or 'staebl'.

To solve an anagram such as 'SOILVENITE' is even more difficult, for a child just does not know where to begin. There is more in solving an anagram or jumbled word than just being able to spell. It is a specific and trained ability to look at words in a new and special way and is one that is *not helpful* to learning to spell.

Words must be found in the sequence of the presented letters of the word. We must, therefore, teach children to look for 'ten' in 'Tottenham', 'sea' in 'Chelsea', 'and' in 'Wanderers', 'right' in 'Brighton'. Football results are fertile ground for this useful activity.

We may also have to produce mnemonics which are often bizarre, but seem to help, e.g. 'Some of the women will come home from Rome'. The teacher who knows what spelling is like can do this quickly and relevantly and it is a most valuable skill and asset.

The dangers of syllabification

When learning a word by Fernald's multi-sensory method or by any Look, Cover, Write, Check technique it is tempting for teachers to break words up into syllables. Fernald thought it important to treat the word as a whole on all occasions, however often the word has to be re-traced. In the end the word has to be written as a unit, so the sooner it is learned in one whole the better. By writing one letter string correctly the likely connection for the next letter string will be provoked. And such practice encourages the child to adopt a more positive attitude towards the words which he feels give him difficulty.

It goes without saying that auditory syllabification, i.e. 'Sound it out, bit by bit' is disastrous to successful spelling, since at each 'bit' a new set of alternatives is presented – all possible but only one correct. By learning the sequence of the word *as a whole*, visually and kinaesthetically, these possibilities are eliminated. There is nevertheless a case to be made for the supportive use of morphemic information, particularly with older children.

Use of morphemic information in learning to spell

The English orthography, as Chomsky (1970) tells us is a near optimal system for representing meaning and not merely sound. This helps reading but not spelling unless we make use of a morphemic strategy. Morphemes are not syllables. They are the smallest units of meaning in the language, and we do not get at them by sound but by sense. Children must disregard sound, and go straight to meaning and letter string. They can write 'soft', so they can manage 'soften'. They can spell words with prefixes such as 'un' and 'dis', in 'unnecessary' and 'dissatisfied', because they know the morphemes 'un' and 'dis' as letter strings. They disregard sound and attend to meaning in writing 'helped' not 'helpt'. They may, as

Thomas (1982) points out, overgeneralise and write a 'virtuous error' such as 'mist' for 'missed'. It is just another case for dismissing 'sound' as a way into spelling.

The importance of developing a kind of imagery, and of increasing the span of apprehension

The catching of spelling occurs also in the context of the caring parent who not only directs the child to what is there in the printed words around him, but who further helps him to take account of events that are not occurring at that precise moment.

The mother who reviews the day's experiences in conversation with the child, who relates 'what we did when we went to Grandma's' with 'what we shall be doing when we go next week', is developing a form of imagery. She may then go a step further in conversation with the child and ask, 'Where did we go first when we went to the zoo?' or 'in the supermarket?' 'Where did we go next?' 'and next?' She is developing, in a very broad sense, sequencing and serial reconstruction.

She is increasing the child's span of reconstruction and ultimately of apprehension, so that he can retell longer and longer sequential journeyings, reviewing and predicting these serially. She is preparing him in all kinds of ways for literacy, as we shall see in the next section of this chapter. But one thing she is doing is to help him to focus on, image and organise larger and larger chunks of material.

The suggestion was made in the last chapter that we learn to spell by looking intently and with interest at words and at sequences to letters within words, and by recalling what we have looked at. Now recall, whether immediate or after a little time, invokes a kind of imagery, and the shorter the exposure and the longer the word exposed, the more the child has to rely on imaging in some way.

There may well be initially an organic structural basis to

48

imagery, yet it does seem as if imagery changes its mode as we develop, particularly in the case of abstract thinkers. It is possible that our preferred form of imagery develops as we mature, from a more generalised system which may or may not have stronger emphases, visual, auditory or kinaesthetic. Bruner *et al.* (1966) quoted research showing that children with high imagery were better than those with low imagery in associating words with pictures, and this is a task very similar to spelling, since it is associating the look of a word with what the word depicts. But Hebb (1968) went on to suggest that the difference between those who have little imaging and those who have much may be not a difference in the mechanism of imaging, but in the way the image is retrieved. Hebb called this 'imaging' a 'serial reconstruction', that is to say the reconstituting of what has been exposed for a very short space of time. There seems to be as much in the way of motor activity to this as there is when we perceive. Hebb talked about part-perceptions being punctuated by eye-movements. This is rather like putting pieces of a jigsaw together as we examine a picture or a scene. Imaging seems to be rather like that. We are fitting together part-images of what have been part-perceptions in a kind of imaged jigsaw, fitting together part-images, but not usually imaging the picture as a whole. We move, as in looking at a picture or a scene, from one bit of the picture to another and we seem to do the same when imaging a picture or a scene (or indeed a word!) The fact that imaging is so like perceiving is highly relevant to spelling.

In the first place, as Hebb says, the child cannot read back words in imagery as quickly as he can read from the printed word, and of course imaginal reading is basic to spelling. The incompleteness of such imaging is symptomatic of spelling difficulty. The child can part-image a word but he can then be held up when a new fixation does not produce a clear image. We wonder why this is so, and whether, in the earlier perception of the word, he was not directed to subsequent parts of the word – particularly to what has traditionally been known as 'hard spots', i.e. letter sequences with acceptable and reasonable alternatives. The writer's research sees this as plausible since the kind of rational correction technique (to be discussed in Chapter 5) which is entirely concerned with attention to hard spots is conducive to good spelling.

Second, attending to serial probability of words, that is to common sequences perceived peripherally in reading and in daily life, facilitates imaging; particularly what has been exposed for a very short space of time. This ability to reconstitute words can unquestionably be improved by training and practice. It will be remembered that given two weeks' training, Radaker (1963) found that after one year the 'imagery' trained groups scored significantly higher on spelling tests than did the control group, showing that such training succeeds in improving spelling performance over longer periods of time, *whatever is inherent in such an exercise* in the way of intent and intention to reproduce. For as a child focusses on a word with intent, he tracks the pattern of the word with his eye, and/or his finger so that there is inevitably some kind of kinaesthetic imagery involved. This is of the utmost value when he does reproduce it. He thus progresses, first through the word in front of him, and then when it is covered up, attends to, and is therefore able to recall, the structure of these letter patterns as he reconstitutes them in letter-by-letter structure.

Ehri (1980, p. 388) put this another way in observing that 'orthographic images can be scanned like real words seen in print, that they include all of the letters in a word's spelling, not just boundary letters or letters mapping into sounds, and that silent letters have a special status in these images' and that these are likely to resemble single conventional forms rather than phonetic variants.

Sloboda (1980, p. 240) suggests that this improvement in spelling was 'contingent on concentrated attention to words rather than on the imagery as such'. He also points out that practising imaging improves subsequent spelling performance. That is not to say that children actually 'use' imagery in their spelling behaviour once the practice sessions are over. He, therefore, endeavoured to find a task involving spelling which would be helped by imagery but where no specific instructions to 'image' were given. He found, as always, that there are indeed individual differences in the use of visual imagery in spelling, and that those who use visual imagery are better at counting (not estimating) the letters in imaged words, but that these were not necessarily good spellers. He concludes that imagery is important in the actual moment when the spelling is *produced*, not in the process by which it is learned.

This seems to be very much in line with Hebb's concept, with the retrievability of the image, rather than the imaging itself. A nine year-old boy was asked by the writer how he was learning the words. He replied, 'I see it on the inside of my eyelids.' When he produced a word he had thus learned, it was obviously by careful retrieval of something he was reconstituting mentally – part-images of former part-perceptions, I guess!

As well as looking at it with intent, he is looking at it with intention to reproduce it, which is why his finger moving along the word and his kinaesthetic imagery are so important. As Martin (1976, p. 213) advises, 'Let your hand help your memory by writing the words down.' His intention to reproduce is because he has been challenged to do this and knows he CAN reproduce a word as a whole. His success is wholly reinforcing. There is indeed evidence that what most strongly influences the catching of spelling is how well a child can see and reproduce a word. Poor spellers in the primary school, or later, can see and reproduce a word if they try, but they have just never challenged themselves or been challenged to make the attempt. It is vital that we use every opportunity for them to be so challenged.

That vision plays a large part in good spelling has been shown in the large number of poor spellers who have reported that they had some defect of vision. Spache (1940) collected reported cases where improvements in reading and spelling followed correction of vision. Though defective vision does not inevitably handicap an individual in spelling – everyone with poor eyesight is not a poor speller – yet it looks as if some specific defects of eyesight, rather than the general visual condition, do affect spelling.

Poor spellers, for example, have frequently been observed to have a small memory span for visually presented material. Spache collected evidence of this from a number of sources, suggesting that limitations in the visual field affected the magnitude of the visual span and might account for the tendency to perceive in small units. It is possible that if the visual field is limited for some time, the child, like a horse in blinkers, sees only a small area at a time. This could explain the smaller visual memory span found in poor spellers (Spache 1940).

It is increase in the length of span that can be apprehended from a single glance at a sentence or a phrase that is important and teachers can, in numerous ways, bring this about. A class of infants was observed copying, letter by letter, from the blackboard the following message to take home, 'We must not bring drinks with our packed lunches.' This is another example of infant teachers losing an opportunity. A short message like this, written out on the board and removed, and written again in short exposures, is making all the demands of looking with intent, interest and intention to reproduce that are basic to spelling and in a practical and short-lived situation.

There are many variations on this kind of technique. Some teachers write the word they wish to teach on paper which, when held up to the light, reveals the word. When put down on the table, the child cannot see the word and can, therefore, not copy it. There are various forms of 'magic slate' where an opaque sheet overlies carbon paper and words can be very easily removed or superimposed.

There is a simple kind of technique practised by many good infant teachers quoted by, for example, Luke, as early as 1931. This was a game of 'catching' and writing words from 'flash cards'. This is, incidentally, an excellent training in looking and reproducing words as wholes and one we could well follow with older children, increasing the length of the words exposed and thus extending the span of what they can take in and reconstitute before writing the word. A traditional children's game which increases the span of apprehension is Kim's Game, where a number of objects is displayed in a group and then hidden, and the children recall as many as possible. As the number is increased, so, too, is the span of apprehension. This can occur with letter sequences displayed visually before being displayed within words that look the same however they sound. This is also a practice which can be exploited by good computer programming in spelling.

To summarise then, imaging seems to consist of the retrieving and fitting together of sequences of letter strings that have previously been perceived as a sequence of part-perceptions. Increasing the number of such sequences facilitates writing from memory. It is through techniques such as exposing words and lengthening sequences of words in one form or another for children to catch and write that they develop this ability not only to image, but to retrieve, reconstitute and reproduce what has been presented.

Intentional communication and handwriting

Speaking and writing are the productive skills that bring real pleasure to the mother of a young child for they spring from the child himself. Certainly she rejoices when he begins to talk and again when he begins to write, for he is spinning words and ideas again when he begins to write.

It is, indeed, a perennial delight to a mother when her child puts pencil or felt-tip to paper, especially when, as so often happens, he 'writes' in a wavy line from left to right, and covers the paper with a simulated message of wavy lines. Sometimes he intersperses his writing with the initial of his own name or other letters he has picked up, and the mother, who gently directs his writing to counter-clockwise movements and to beginning at the top of vertical strokes, is preparing her child for what is so important in spelling, namely good handwriting.

This is another attribute of the caring and concerned mother, and one that might well affect her child's future writing. It is a rudimentary skill that the child is beginning to acquire and one which it is crucial that teachers of young children need to consider seriously from the very beginning.

What affects spelling very considerably is handwriting, and what affects it in particular is carefulness in handwriting. Surprisingly, the careful writer tends to be the swift writer and swift handwriting greatly influences spelling ability. Indeed as Jarman (1979) points out, legibility and flow are far more important than neatness, and for these the teacher is wholly responsible.

Aesthetic considerations apart, handwriting would seem to require little more than the development and control of fine muscular movements and familiarity with conventional direction. Yet in a concise and serious study of the development of handwriting Thomassen and Teulings (1983) comment that skilled writing movements are so commonplace that one is inclined to overlook their complexity. In the late 1960s, the writer monitored the handwriting of a whole age-group of children through the last three years of the primary school. One interesting fact that emerged was that 23 per cent of the writing of nine-year-old children was 'barely legible'. Much of this handwriting was poor in that it was badly-formed. These children had just not been taught to form letters correctly, that is, according to convention. Now, as every infant teacher knows, the conventions in print are simple:

> 'All round letters are anti-clockwise.
> All straight letters begin at the top.'

It is a comparatively easy skill to teach, but, unfortunately, it is easy enough to stop watching a child once one has taught him the conventions. And as soon as one stops watching, a child reverts to ad hoc, random letter formation, which is as often wrong as it is right! A teacher must watch a child form letters correctly until the habit is established. This means that young children should not be inveigled into writing too much *until*

54

they can form letters correctly. This sounds prescriptive and didactic and it is intended to be. If children are to write legibly at a later date, it is crucial that the Infant teacher watches each child write and makes certain that the correct habits are laid down firmly and permanently. This implies the need for certainty of letter shapes where the writer is producing some form of joined writing in which the letters are produced in a continuous flow. This allows him to concentrate on the letter pattern and word structure rather than the letter formation.

Bryant and Bradley (1983, p. 177) show the success children have when they write out words at the same time as they spell them. 'With this method', Bradley quotes from her earlier writing, 'backward readers are able to remember and reproduce the spelling of difficult and irregular words quite successfully and over a long period of time.' She confirms that establishing writing patterns helps them to remember spelling.

There is no question that children with swift motor control write groups of letters, for example, 'ing' 'ean' 'est', in a connected form and this is the basis of knowledge about which letters stick together. This is the crux of spelling ability, for handwriting and spelling go hand in hand. They are interdependent, for handwriting which is correctly formed has been practised and reinforced in the joined-up writing of conventional letter strings. Quality of handwriting is highly correlated with spelling attainment, so also is speed of handwriting, for it is a myth that the slow writer is the careful writer and vice versa. The slow writer is often one who is uncertain of letter formation, who is faced with a decision every time he comes to a fresh letter and, as often as not, makes a random attempt at the letter he is writing. The swift writer is one who is certain of letter formation and, as a bonus, is certain of letter sequences so that he can make a reasonable attempt at a word he may never have written before. The word flows from the end of his pencil. Indeed Thomassen and Teulings (1983) are of the opinion that comparing correct and incorrect versions of letter strings should help us to know much more about the nature of handwriting development.

Spelling in the Infant School

A strong case can be made for teaching 'joined-up' writing from the beginning of a child's school life. There is, of course, the problem that it is somewhat different from the printed form the children are meeting in books and in the outside world, but it is only in the joining of the letters that it differs, and correspondence techniques quickly take over. The advantages are many:

1 There is no change 'from print to cursive' in the junior years. Hence, there is never any question of 'low status' as there is in children who have not yet started 'joined-up' writing.
2 Words are separate from the beginning and the concept of 'a word' is acquired from the time a child begins to write.
3 Correct letter formation is ensured from the beginning. Too many children just 'pick-up' 'joined-up' writing in the junior years with little help in the conventional letter formation that is crucial to legibility.
4 Spelling is helped, since letter strings are necessarily connected – 'ame' 'ough' 'per', etc.

The teaching of 'joined-up' writing on school entry is a debatable question, but one that should be discussed very seriously if children's invented spellings are quickly and painlessly to develop into spelling according to our English conventional orthography and children are to be free to write spontaneously, expressively attending to what is important in the composition of what they are writing.

Whether using joined-up writing or script-print, well-formed writing can be taught easily and effectively from the age of five and within the process of learning to write from memory. This is being demonstrated in an on-going exercise with five-year-old children in Scotland (Cripps 1983b). The wise use of Breakthrough to Literacy is in capitalising upon the children's own utterances reproduced in the Breakthrough

sentence holder, by writing these, and by the teacher expecting the children to write their sentences from memory instead
of blindly copying. This is integral to such work with infants,
for this involves the children in looking with intent and intention to reproduce. The fact that this occurs so rarely is yet
another example of many infant teachers' lost opportunities in
teaching spelling.

As Kail (1979) pointed out, seven-year-old children knew
that memory tasks call for some special effort and activity, and
knew the difference between 'just look' and 'memorise this',
but they did not know what to do to help themselves. Learning
to write from memory is something they need to be taught.
The children's first comments in the Scottish study when their
sentence makers were turned over were defeatist – 'I can't
copy unless I can see it' – which would have said much for their
future learning habits, had it been left at that. These children
were given a further opportunity of 'looking at' their sentences: 'Look carefully at each word, turn the sentence maker
over and then write the word.' This was the beginning of the
Look-Cover-Write-Check routine in the context of the Breakthrough to Literacy material. The 'freedom to write' generated
by this learning to write from memory is putting these children
in a position where their purposeful writing for a particular
audience, their intentional communication, their forays into
authorship, are not hampered by having to bother about
spelling.

Children who have learned to write words with reasonably
correct spelling and with well-formed handwriting are freed to
write whatever they want to write. They can make a reasonable guess at a new word which is as yet only in their own
passive, not their active, spoken or written vocabularies, i.e.
they have heard the word, but have never spoken it, let alone
written it, but they want to try it out. So their attempts at the
word are good attempts, since they are according to precedent
in our own language. These children are free not only to write
purposefully, for their own needs, but to 'conference' with
their teachers without being distracted, as so many are, by the

demands of spelling, since it is not automatised. As we shall see in the next section, poor spelling is a hidden and un-acknowledged problem for many teachers developing children's writing through the important procedures of con-ferencing, drafting, redrafting and editing.

Intentional communication

The roots of literacy are in shared activity. The talk, the reading, the directing of attention, the reviewing of, and pre-dicting of, joint activities – these are all the ground from which literacy grows. And from the very earliest stages, it is 'inten-tional communication' with another person that is central to language development (McShane 1980). A child's productive language in speech is infinitely rewarding to the mother. Indeed, she gets very anxious if her child is not beginning to speak. Productive skills are more important to her than the receptive skills of listening and reading, for with productive skills, speaking and writing, she hears her child generating new and original utterances and texts that may never have been produced before. She is amazed. When a child speaks, he is directing his mother's attention; he is attempting to regulate her; he is initiating that 'intentional communication' with another person that is central to language development (McShane 1980), and it is effective, for she responds. Not only is he regulating her orally, but he is, very soon, doing just that in writing. He is leaving her little messages, and messages not only to her but to Teeth Fairies and Father Christmas and other such munificent beings. It is the accepting, the responding, the encouraging and the seizing of opportunities such as these for spoken and written communication that is so promising for his future literacy.

The evidence for this is in the quality of such purpose-ful writing, for notes and letters written as 'intentional communication' are more legible and the spelling nearer the conventional English orthography than in other contexts. This is necessarily so, since for the child, the message is important and must be clear enough to read; the message MUST get across. And after all, we only have to remember what care adults take when writing letters of application for posts, that their spelling is perfect and their handwriting completely legible. So in school also, we respond to, we encourage and we devise opportunities for purposeful writing and rejoice in it as 'intentional communication' for we, as teachers, are a privileged audience. Durrell is quoted by Graves (1978, p. 8) as saying 'We have known for years the child's first urge is to write and not read and we haven't taken advantage of this fact. We have underestimated the power of the output languages like speaking and writing.'

In the DES Primary School Survey, *Language Performance in Schools* (1981) we read that in most cases writing that was judged to be excellent in terms of style and content was also judged to be proficient in terms of spelling and vice versa. There is clearly a desire for careful and pleasing presentation of what a child feels it is important for him to write and it is this motivation to present, to redraft and to 'publish' that is behind the exciting work going on in junior and secondary schools in the area of children's writing.

Frank Smith (1982) distinguishes between transcription (the secretarial) and composition (the performative) skills. Conferencing is concerned with the performative, but is dependent upon the secretarial skills which must have been taught if the teacher, no less than the child, is to be free to conference. It is in the context of what has come to be known as 'conferencing' (Graves, 1983), when the teacher 'visits' the children as they write, that the problem of spelling really arises. It is assumed by the teacher that, at this point, surface skills of spelling, handwriting, layout and appearance are not priorities, and this is understandable, as the objective in 'conferencing' is to facilitate the child's own meaning, his own story structure, within a predictable setting and atmosphere in which he can talk privately about his writing product.

Similarly, at the secondary stage, Binns (1980) is concerned with encouraging children to move on from the initial steps of working from speech to writing, so that they are capable of drafting and redrafting, editing and self-correcting. It is here, however, that we come face to face with the problem of spelling. At all stages, we find that teachers, as well as children, are worried, even preoccupied with the problems of spelling. Indeed, Kamler and Kilarr (1983, pp. 201, 202) state 'This is not to say the teacher ignores spelling. Quite the contrary. The teacher *looks for opportunities* to refine the spelling skills of the child during conferences.' Frequently, in practice, they spend an inordinate amount of time in discussion about spelling and this is not what is intended at all in conferencing. These are times when the surface skills of spelling are not to be in the forefront of the interaction between teacher and child. The important thing is the drive towards cognitive clarity, which has to be serviced by the technical skills, not dominated by them. Only too often, teachers get these the wrong way round which interferes with the true purpose of the conference.

There are two ways out of this dilemma. One is by teaching spelling systematically, with sound visuo-motor strategies from the very beginning, through the learning of letter strings and the generalisation of these, and from teaching young children to write from memory. The problem of spelling would not then impede the activity of the conference about content, argument, appropriateness of style, etc.

There is another way of dealing with this very real dilemma in which teachers find themselves and in which they appeal for help. It is that when, in a 'conference', a child is faced with a spelling problem, the teacher should, instead of discussing possible ways of spelling a particular word, merely write the word on a piece of paper on the child's table saying, 'It's like this – look at it' and then remove it. Since the child wants to spell the word correctly, he will look carefully and in so doing retain it. This is NOT the time to spend on the teaching of spelling. But this is not to say that there should not be systematic and rational spelling instruction at other points in the curriculum.

It is reported (Graves, 1984) that Jamie took fifteen minutes to write 'A tornado went by here now', most of that time having been spent on trying to invent a spelling for 'tornado'. Was this an important discovery exercise for Jamie? Or was this time that would have been more usefully spent in conference with the teacher developing the form of his own theme, since it can be assumed that he had much more to say about the tornado than appeared in the bald statement he did make.

There are many instances of teachers of secondary pupils spending much too long a time discussing a spelling, which could have been shown in a few seconds and the time saved spent on more profitable discussion.

It is not in the first few months of school that formal conferencing takes place. In the very early days, the child is writing and inventing spellings for what he wants to write in his story or diary. It is at this point that, instead of waiting for these invented spellings to develop from crude patterns to greater refinement and to merge into conventional spelling, infant teachers seize the opportunity of teaching the child to write from memory the words they need. Their writing vocabulary is not large, but large enough to include many high frequency words, words like 'when' and 'said' and 'bought' which will not easily develop from invented letter strings, unlike 'whe', 'aid' and 'ough' which, once they can write them from memory, will be generalised to other words such as 'where', 'whether', 'paid' and 'enough'.

There are, as Bereiter and Scardamalia (in press) point out, two main difficulties children have to face in writing. One difficulty is in the overall burden of things which have to be kept in mind when writing, (the information processing load) in which, of course, spelling bears a very heavy part. The other difficulty is in the child's structuring of his written production (what they call 'discourse schemata'). They see the writer as a kind of air traffic controller directing all this!

To exploit and adapt the analogy further, the controller can only be helped by, and can only rely on the preliminary servicing of the aircraft (the parallel is in giving the child a reliable, written spelling system so that he need not try to 'invent' possible spellings as the plane, as it were, flies in). The controller is secure in his knowledge that his instruments work!

The controller can then attend to the variables. In the case of writing this will be to the imaginative structuring of what he wants to write. If at this point, his instruments fail (or the child is baulked in his spelling), the controller himself takes over quickly, and supplies the resource without taking his attention from the structuring of his writing.

There is no questioning the fact that spelling is only an instrument for writing, and that if it is serviceable, the child can attend to the vital elements of composition, planning, sustained production, memory search, structuring, know-ledge-telling, expression of emotion, and of course revising, redrafting and editing.

Bereiter and Scardamalia recall Vygotsky's emphasis that the role of the adult in promoting learning often consists of taking over part of a complex process and transferring it to the child. This is certainly true of conferencing with the child about his writing. But the part of the complex process most easily and felicitously taken over by the teacher is in first promoting, and then lightly servicing, spelling as a sound reliable basis which frees the child to write, unburdened by the heaviest part of his information processing load.

Acquiring secretarial skills preparatory to performative activity

In order that children should be free to write, and not to be tempted to write an easier alternative just because they cannot spell the more precise word they want to write, and in order that they should be free to attend to the important business of conferencing with the teacher, namely the moves towards cognitive clarity, it is crucial that as many of the support systems become automatic as early as possible. These are the support systems that Bereiter and Scardamalia (in press) see as over-burdening the writer's information processing channel. They supply the secretarial skills which can be acquired very early in school life. If they are acquired through the use of 'Breakthrough to Literacy' and through learning the words the child wants to write quickly and easily the objective of attention to the performative side of writing will be easily achieved.

We are reminded by Hildreth (1956) of the close relationship between growth in language and progress in spelling, and that spelling is learned by constant practice in writing. Yet ability in spelling cannot be acquired by just writing – as well we know from the free writing of young children. Some method must be found whereby children can with the least possible withdrawal of attention from their creative writing be faced with the correct spelling of the word they need.

Class dictionaries, but more often individual dictionaries, are used in schools to satisfy this need. A child asks for a word and it is written in his individual dictionary. He copies it into his free writing and continues to write. There is a speedy return to the child's creative work, but no sooner has the word been written in the composition, than the word is, as it were, wiped out mentally, in the same way that we look up a telephone number, dial the number and wipe out the number so effectively that if we are given a wrong number, we have to look up the number again in the directory. In the same way, a child, having written the word and wiped out the memory of it, may forget it to the point of asking the teacher for that same word again the same day. It is necessary, therefore, to *direct* the child's attention to the word that has been written, and to insist on his writing it in his composition, as a whole, from memory. Surely this is the essence of Fernald's technique. For normally-learning creative children finger-tracing of words on cards and allocation of cards to a file is a cumbersome business. Provided that the child looks carefully at the word that has been written and closes his personal dictionary before writing it in his composition, the learning of the word has been initiated. The intention to remember has been retained, if only for the space of time it takes to write the word. There is a theoretical issue here in that immediate checking has not been catered for. There is a calculated risk that a word may have been written incorrectly, especially if the span of the word is longer than about six letters. The practice of taking the personal dictionary and checking the words asked for and acquired during the past lesson would partly remedy this. In any case the first learning should be consolidated in the formal learning of the child's own needed and asked-for words, at a later time. Thus, this learning is subsidiary to, and an integral part of, the child's 'creative writing'.

It is, of course, essential that the word should be acquired with no delay so that the sentence continues to flow without interruption. It is important to establish habits, for example, of the child presenting the 'dictionary' open at the correct page, so that the teacher can write the word quickly and the child look at it and *learn* the look of it as he returns to his desk. In a class-room climate where writing is encouraged by an appreciative audience the teacher's quick response avoids delay, and in the writer's experience, there has never been known what is so inimical to lively learning and expression, a queue! To avoid having to ask for all words, certain common words can, of course, be made available in word-lists, and common nouns can be acquired from a picture dictionary.

Active self-testing is perhaps the most effective method of learning material such as spelling, and for the consolidation of this learning the teacher, and later the children themselves, can write the words asked for in a notebook with folded pages to provide space where the child can test and re-test himself without copying, since the word is hidden before the child writes the word. This avoids the need for the formulation of elaborate rules, as repeated examples of words within the child's vocabulary provide the repetition of examples necessary. Often it is only when a rule is pointed out to a habitually good speller that doubts begin to occur. This avoids the need for a test-study procedure, as the children will only be learning

64

the words they do not know, yet need to know, and recognise that they need to know, and are therefore motivated to learn. This avoids, too, the use of carefully graded word-lists suited to a certain age, as the words are in the children's own idiom. Some children, who are less able linguistically, will ask for less sophisticated words than children who are verbally adventurous, but they will be learning to write the words *they* need. And spelling is an essential skill only in so far as we want to write. A good speller who never puts pen to paper is like a good linguist who never speaks or reads the language he knows.

Some spelling errors will occur, however. Children will invent a word. They will, engrossed in the development of their story, flow on without asking, and memory images can deceive. It is so easy in reading creative writing for the teacher to notice the *errors*, not the strength and vividness of composition, and easier still when wielding the red pencil. To avoid too much attention to the errors, and to co-operate with the child in producing a well-presented and correct piece of writing, the child could write his stories and diary in pencil, so that the teacher can rub out the spelling errors, preferably in the child's presence. He himself should fill in the words which the teacher has written correctly in his dictionary. What is more, the intention to spell a word correctly may well transfer some habit of care and satisfaction in the production of an orderly and well-presented piece of writing. This is an integrated approach that demands rigours of learning and execution, though not at the expense of creative writing. For, as Hildreth (1956, p. 34) writes, 'Teachers should not think of incidental learning and integrated teaching as excluding systematic, well-organized drill. Rather from the child's attempts to write will come the need for systematic word study.'

The importance of children developing a firm strategy for learning new words

In the literature about spelling Arvidson (1963) and the writer recall the kind of techniques advocated by Horn (1919) which is basically a 'look-cover-write-check' routine. In this the child is trained to look carefully at the structure of the word, endeavour to memorise it, and then make an attempt to reproduce the whole word. If, after checking, the attempt is different from the original then the procedure is repeated again.

This technique should also help prevent letter-by-letter copying which is unacceptable, because it is ineffective for learning. When writing a new word it is also important for the child not to *sound* or *spell out* the word letter by letter, but, instead, write it from memory *saying* the whole word slowly as he writes. In this way, he is writing the letter pattern as he is saying the word and hence becoming aware of the visual and graphic relationship of its structure. It is also worth noting why 'spelling out' is a poor strategy of learning:

(a) It emphasises the auditory rather than the visual input.
(b) It is an uneconomic way of learning in that every
    word has to be repeated.
(c) Letter-by-letter reciting prompts useless alphabetic
    associations, and i.e. names of letters.
(d) It is motivationally unsound in that it is so far removed
    from genuine purposes in writing, for we only need to
    spell in order to write.

How to learn a new word

It is essential that children be taught the following routine for learning a new word: (This is the kind of technique advocated by Horn (1919) and Arvidson (1963).)

1 LOOK   at the word carefully and in such a way that you
                will remember what you have seen.
2 COVER   the word so that you cannot see it.
3 WRITE   the word from *memory*, saying it softly to
                yourself as you are writing.
4 CHECK what you have written. If you have not written
                the word correctly, do not alter it, instead go
                back and repeat all these steps again,

or, as Nancy Martin (1976, p. 213) writes, 'let your hand help your eye and your memory by writing the words down. The fingers of trained typists do much of their owners' spelling for them . . . look at a word you want to learn, then shut your eyes and try to see it in print in your mind's eye.'

This chapter has been concerned with teaching children to catch what favoured children have caught, by directing attention to letter strings, by exercising imaging and increasing the span which can be imaged and reproduced and by laying down well-formed handwriting – all this in order to free children to write and to benefit from the exciting renaissance of interest in children's writing in conferencing, drafting and redrafting, editing and publishing of children's writing.

Spelling and handwriting are the servants of this freedom. Historical and current approaches to the teaching of spelling will next be reviewed, since from the roots of the incidental/ systematic controversy has grown our present theory and practice.

4

Historical approaches to the teaching of spelling

Traditional approaches to the teaching of spelling have been concerned with what rather than with how to teach. The 'how' has been a much more sophisticated concern in the history of education, than the 'what'. So first we will return to the 'what' which has indeed been a major preoccupation with research workers in spelling.

Long before the incidental learning controversy (which is very much a 'how' question) teachers were concerned with what words children should learn and they were making word-lists to this end. One, dated 1882, but found in a primary school cupboard in the 1950s, includes in one lesson the words, 'bissextile', 'decennial', 'chimerical', and 'chalybeate'! Such lists are obviously not derived from children's language either spoken or written. Indeed it was not until 1911 that words ceased to be selected arbitrarily and were selected on the basis of the frequency with which they occurred. In that year Eldridge recorded the 6,000 most common English words from newspapers. In the next few years counts were made particularly of the spelling vocabulary of personal and business letters (Ayres, 1913) because here spelling deficiency was most embarrassingly revealed. The following year the first list derived from children's writing (Cook and O'Shea, 1914) appeared. This has been succeeded through the years by many counts taken from children's writing of compositions and letters, culminating in the 1964 word count of children's spontaneous writing by Edwards and Gibbon in their Leicestershire Vocabulary Survey.

Since counts of words used by children in their own writing are the most real evidence of what children want to write, it is obviously on these that the spelling lists should be based. Not many, however, are based directly on children's writing. One of the most extensive and thorough is that by Rinsland (1945), who examined and graded more than 6 million words in 100,000 scripts of children, from 416 American cities. The resulting spelling list contained only words appearing more than three times in any one grade. This list was further graded by Hildreth (1953) who noted how words became so highly specialised after the first 2,000 or so that it was difficult to determine which to include in primary school spelling lists. Johnston's list (1950) from children's writing was confined to the hundred words he found that children were most likely to mis-spell. In 1955, the Scottish Council for Research in Education took a much more positive line by producing a spelling vocabulary, derived from a count of the words in 70,000 compositions written freely by seven to twelve-year-old pupils in Scottish schools, on topics selected to suit their interests.

Many lists, however, have been prepared, often subjectively, from other sources, often remote from children's writing needs, from e.g. adults' correspondence or adults' reading material, as was the famous 30,000-word list of Thorndike and Lorge (1944). To do this is to teach children to spell words that adults, not they themselves, write. No wonder Fernald wrote 'Formal word lists will always fail to supply the particular word a person should learn at a particular time' (1943, p. 210). Words which children are learning from derived lists may well be the words they will not need till they themselves are adult and writing formal letters, for it has been found that there is little in common between the vocabulary of children's writing and that of adults' formal literary writing. Hildreth (1953) confirmed earlier findings that derived spelling word lists were very different in content from the words used in children's writing. She also found that word-forms that children use may be different from the forms appearing in derived lists, e.g. children make more frequent use of the past tense and of the plural form than the present tense and singular form that appear in the lists.

If a list is derived it is important to know its source. Apart from those already mentioned as having stemmed from word counts of children's writing, most spelling lists have been derived from word counts, particularly from Thorndike's earlier list. Washburne's (1923) spelling curriculum was based partly on Thorndike's lists, though in part on adult correspondence and children's compositions. Breed (1925) answered, 'What words should children be taught to spell?' from sixteen different sources, eleven of which were adult. Even Schonell's familiar 'Essential Spelling List' (1932), the one most widely used in English schools, is a subjective list derived from Horn (adults' writing, 1926) and Thorndike (adults' reading material, 1921), though here there is an empirically based relationship with well standardised norms of spelling ability, i.e. with what children can, not necessarily with what they want to spell.

Gates's (1937) list was derived from a count of words in twenty-five spelling books used in American schools. Bixler (1940) produced a standard spelling scale from eight sources and then the popular *Key Words to Literacy* (McNally and Murray, 1968), was a derived list, but intended as a minimum sight vocabulary to be used in the teaching of reading and not primarily intended as a spelling list.

From such lists, the Bureau of Curriculum Research of the Board of Education in the City of New York compiled a list of 5,000 words graded into ten frequency levels. From this State list, the New Zealand Council of Educational Research list of 2,700 words had been originally derived (1963). But this was only a starting point. This list was widely examined by inspectors, college lecturers and teachers and checked against a number of well-known derived lists as well as word counts of New Zealand children's writing. This was later published as the Alphabetical Spelling List (Arvidson, 1963) and was one of the few at that time to present explicit instructions as to how to learn.

Many spelling books have been produced with lists devised in devious ways, but few until recently said much about how to set about learning. Students presented with nonsense words to learn to spell soon find it necessary to evolve an efficient method. Most students depend on associative clues and mnemonics; rarely do they depend on oral recitation. Must children, inexperienced in organisation of material to be learned and unaware of the laws of learning, be expected to evolve by trial and error an economical method of learning spelling lists?

Learning to spell, without being given instructions as to how to learn, leads to haphazard techniques which may well be inappropriate to a particular child's idiosyncrasies of perception and imagery. It may, for example, lead children to spell alphabetically. This is a time-honoured method, but it involves an unnecessarily complicated sequence of events. The child learns the word by reading it and repeating the alphabetic names of the letters. He writes it by first saying the name of each letter in turn and writing it before reading the completed word. He is using two distinct codes, the alphabetic name code and the 'sounds', and one does not immediately evoke the other. If we hear a word spelt by alphabetic letter names, the word is not immediately meaningful. We have to translate the names into sounds. If the word is spelt by sounds, long before it is finished, we have leapt mentally, with immediacy of perception, to complete the whole word with almost certainly a visual, and probably an auditory image, concomitant with the meaning of the word. This is only one example of the precariousness of leaving children to learn uninstructed by trial and error.

Fulton pointed out in 1914, in the days when spelling lists of dubious origin and derivation abounded, that pupils following a systematic method make much greater progress and retain their learning better than those given no directions for learning to spell. Twenty years later Alice Watson (1935) was recommending that children should be taught to master efficient techniques for self-teaching. Only too often children, given a list without a method, read over the list rapidly or recite the names of the letters, names that have no immediate relation to the overall sound of the word. A somewhat more sophisticated way of learning is to learn syllabically, sounding the syllables one by one. But to rely wholly on auditory memory is to put oneself in a position of uncertainty when faced with the alternatives presented by even regular phonemic words, and it is a pity to rely on a method that breaks down just when it is most needed. Unsupported by other sensory inroads, this is a precarious means to spelling.

It was not until 1962 that the linguist Fries (1962, pp. 171–84) enumerated and described spelling patterns:

(a) One-syllable words with the general shape of consonant-vowel-consonant, e.g. mad.
(b) Spelling-patterns using the final 'e' to differentiate them from 'a', made. (These to cover a large part of the active practices of English.)
(c) A number of important spelling-patterns of much more limited application, involving the varied doubled vowels.

These three major sets of spelling-pattern form the basis of the modern English spelling we have to learn. We must, he points out, as does Torbe (1977), 'learn to spell the unstressed syllables of each word, e.g. sound patterns with the same vowel phoneme in the final syllable, orphan, silken, sojourn, dragon, handsome, etc.' 'Most misspellings', Torbe writes (1977, p. 8), 'in words of more than one syllable have been found to occur in the unstressed syllable, especially in the vowel.' These are all possibilities that children must be aware can occur, before they can learn when they should occur, and it is only relating these with other words containing these unstressed syllables but that look the same, that children learn these, e.g.

orphan	silken	journey
elephant	end	our
alphabet	present	your
	pretend	court
		courteous
		harbour
		favourite

It is, however, not only the unstressed syllable but the middle of the word that presents difficulty.

Jensen (1962) showed that spelling errors occur more often in medial than in the beginning or ending of words, and it is the middle phonemes of words that have quite reasonable alternatives that are the cause of so much difficulty in learning to spell. First the possibilities must be learned. Now to be able to perceive word-form implies knowledge of probable letter sequences through precedents in our spelling system. It will be remembered that Wallach (1963, p. 61) demonstrated that good spellers showed much more transfer of training from familiar to unfamiliar or nonsense words than poor spellers and this, he says, suggests some new implications regarding what one should attempt to teach in order to improve a child's spelling. 'Whereas teaching procedures based on phonetic training have been in use for some time there has been little attempt yet to base training procedures on transfer involving the sequential probability structure of letters.' To effect such transfer, there must occur day by day verbal experiences of every possible variant of spelling pattern in the language. This is where procedures of the kind suggested in Chapter 5 using modern visual media such as television advertising are justified. Children are learning the nonsense of their own language, and it is primarily in an informal manner such as this that such learning occurs. This is where incidental learning is really justified, where children usefully catch the flavour and vagaries of their own language structure, where they are constantly and inevitably receiving the impact of such verbal stimuli in traditional orthography through advertisements, names and signs. Before spelling learning can be really effective, children must be aware of the probable structures of words in their language. There are, of course, less informal ways in which such awareness is brought about. The infant teacher writes on the child's picture captions that the child dictates. He watches and is satisfied with his own verbalisation. The mother reads to her child and the child follows as she reads. The mother and father, as they drive along, read the names of towns, villages and streets and the children articulate the names and words as they see them.

Schonell (1942), of course, pointed out that the visual, auditory and articulatory elements must be 'firmly cemented by writing'. For by writing the attention is focussed and 'helps to bridge the gap between visual and auditory symbols by successive production of the constituent parts of the visual form.' This writing which gives children the 'feel' of the word is vital to correct spelling. As children progress they become less and less aware of the visual, auditory, and articulatory elements, until they achieve the machine-like movement where, as they write, the initial letter initiates the muscular contraction stimulating the second letter in a chain-like series, a chain reaction supplying the whole word. There is such a moment today in using a typewriter or computer in learning to type when, instead of typing letter by letter, the student suddenly in one sweep produces a word. T-h-e is produced in one satisfying, complete unalterable movement. The first letter, t, triggers off the h, the h, the e, and if the typist images the word it may well be in muscular contractions in the fingers involved. It is here that the teacher of typing restrains the student, in the enthusiasm of his new-found skill, from typing each word with a flourish, and stopping at the end of each. In the interests of using the typewriter efficiently, he then attends to the phrase, sentence and paragraph rather than word wholes. The *gestalt* is enlarged and this is achieved by the teacher's insistence on rhythmical typing. It is interesting, incidentally, to speculate on the possible effect on spelling of this insistence on rhythmic technique.

Repeated writing, however much it bridges the gap between visual and auditory symbols, involves auditory and articulatory elements only implicitly. Schonell spoke of 'the absolute necessity of emphasising all means of ingress in learning words, the visual, the auditory and the kinaesthetic'. A child or adult may be handicapped by one rather weak sensory mechanism; he may have poor perceptual grasp of the significance of a word, his imagery may be very one-sided or he may be distracted by other sensory stimuli. If such a child is bombarded by several sensory stimuli supporting each other in emphasising the structure of a word to remember, he will inevitably attend to and learn the word. And this is what Fernald (1943) suggested.

The problem of homophones

There is still the problem of homophones. As Vallins (1965, p. 144) says 'they are a natural and necessary by-product of a spelling that preserves in its symbols the etymological origin of words'.

Only the meaning and the grammar will point the writer to the correct one of the two. The look of the word must be connected with its meaning. This is an example of an aspect of spelling that does not conform to letter-sound conventions. Whenever the wrong alternative is written, at least it can be said to be a 'good error', a 'virtuous error' for it conforms to spelling precedent. For that reason, it is not really necessary for the teacher to correct it. The child who writes 'I mist the bus' is a good speller. He will, in the course of time and experience of the conventions of English grammar, learn to write 'missed' in this context.

It is worth noting here the influence of reading methods on the ability to cope with homophones in spelling. In the writer's research (1970) children taught to read by 'look and say' methods (what is now often termed a 'meaning emphasis') are superior, since the visual aspect of the word is conjured up directly by the meaning and associations of the word.

Talking about homophones, Stubbs (1983, p. 282) reminds us that they are common in English (unlike homographs which look the same but have different sounds and different meanings and are rare words like 'bow' and 'read'). 'Writing', he says 'is designed to be seen and not heard.'

Teaching spelling by rules

Now some children can approach spelling from a much more rational angle than others, and grasp and apply rules earlier and more efficiently than others. Most rules taught come from the teachers' experience, only a few from text-books. Here the great difficulty is in the wording of the rules, for example, 'Words ending in silent "e" drop the "e" when adding a suffix beginning with a vowel, and keep the "e" when adding a suffix beginning with a consonant.' This is the first of four rules framed by Wheat (1932, p. 700) and one which he said was short, simple, easy to learn, remember and use, and had the advantage of covering 23 per cent of the words in the vocabulary he analysed with less than 1 per cent exception. Another rule ran (p. 703) 'monosyllables and words of more than one syllable with the accent on the last syllable, which end in a single consonant preceded by a single vowel, double the final consonant when adding a suffix beginning with a vowel.'

During in-service courses over a thousand teachers were asked to write the word 'benefited'. Of these 51 per cent wrote it correctly, but 29 per cent wrote 'benefitted'. After having the above rule read to them, many changed their spelling from correct to incorrect since they just did not understand the rule!

The length and technicality of such rules are frightening, yet it is often assumed that, by the time the child needs to spell untaught words, he can comprehend and use such rules and this for children still in the stage of concrete operational thinking! This is very questionable since use of technical terms, e.g. noun, plural, singular, suffix, etc. presupposed a mental level far in advance of the use of nouns, plurals, singulars.

It is generally agreed that:

(a) The rule must apply to a large number of words.
(b) It must have few exceptions.
(c) The statement of the rules must be simple and easily comprehended while being sufficiently exact to cover only the appropriate words.

As Foran (1934, p. 141) said, 'If a rule involves unfamiliar terms, it may become a major difficulty in itself and contribute nothing to spelling.'

Reservations about the use of rules

There are many serious and valid reservations about the use of rules in the teaching of spelling, however. 'Before a new rule is introduced,' wrote McLeod (1961, p. 130), 'the following should be borne in mind. Knowledge of a rule serves no useful purpose unless it covers a number of words which might reasonably be expected to be already in the children's spelling vocabulary and embraces also other words likely to be needed which the children may spell by generalization.' No wonder Vallins (1965, p. 15) wrote 'There are no reliable rules and even the guiding principles, of which there are more than we imagine, are apt sometimes to fail and mislead both ear and eye.' McLeod's own research showed that presenting each word separately was a better method than teaching words with the aid of spelling rules where applicable.

Rules, according to Sloboda (1980, p. 232) are just not sufficient for perfect spelling. 'When one looks', he writes, 'at the spelling errors of literate adults one is perhaps seeing the gap between what the rules supply and what, in the case of perfect spellers, is provided by a rapid and accurate form of spelling memory.' In any case, rule-learning and generalisation from rules rather than from letter strings depends upon a developmental level of mental operation that is beyond the level of children still at the stage of concrete operational thinking.

The limitation of rules in the teaching of spelling was highlighted more forcefully by Hanna, Hanna, Hodges and Rudorf (1966) in Simon and Simon (1973) who programmed a computer to spell by using over 200 spelling rules, but the computer just couldn't manage it. Given 17,009 different words to spell it failed with over half, e.g. 'bus' was spelt 'buss', 'team' spelt 'teem', 'coal' was spelt 'cole' and 'tie' as 'ty'! It is probable that most people can spell more than the half that the computer could spell from rules. Indeed, Simon and Simon (1973) reported that ten-year-olds could outspell the computer. For we just do not rely on rules. Everyone knows the rule 'i before e except after c', yet two of the most frequent spelling mistakes in 'O' level papers reported in 1978 by the Associated Examining Board were 'receive' and 'believed'. Presumably the candidates 'knew the rule'. The words were just not automatised as they would have been if, in the primary school, they had learned and overlearned the letter string 'cei' as in 'ceiling', 'receive' and 'deceive' and 'lie' as in 'believe', 'relieve' and 'earlier'! As Simon and Simon (1973, p. 135) stated, 'spelling will only be learned if sufficient visual recognition information is available'. Letter strings are a part of what Jorm (1983) calls a 'mental lexicon' upon which we rely more securely than on rules – what Sloboda (1980) means when he talks about 'a rapid and accurate form of spelling memory' which is what perfect spellers rely on, rather than rules which he says are just not sufficient for perfect spelling.

Test-study/Study-test method

Fernald, as we have seen, maintained that the most satisfactory spelling vocabulary is that supplied by the child himself. She condemns spelling books and word lists for denying the particular word a writer requires at a specific moment. But there is another difficulty about spelling lists in the economy of time and effort for the child. Most spelling lists, both with and without instructions as to how to learn the words, imply 'These words must be learned at a particular stage.' But some of the words will be already known by the children. Some words will be more easily learnt and with less attention on the part of a child than others. There is a 'curve of mastery' for each word. Some children learn a particular word early, some late, some easily, some with difficulty. And, as we have seen, there is considerable progress in learning to spell incidentally from year to year apart from practice in spelling lessons. In fact, Thompson (1930) found that many words are known before they are studied. Of 2,127 words, 25 per cent were spelled correctly before study by 84 per cent of children. It is reasonable then, in presenting a spelling list, for these words to be tested before being learned (Gates, 1931), so that for children, who can already spell some of the words, time is not wasted, effort misdirected, and early success not enjoyed.

If lists are to be learned it would seem economical for the practice suggested by Bernard (1931) and quoted in the Scottish *Studies in Spelling* (1961), to be followed. Children knowing the number of words to be learned should work in pairs, testing each other and learning the required number of words from the series of lists. This is the test-study in contrast to the traditional study-test method. The fact that the writer has not found this in use in any of the schools being studied suggests that this is either a very unwieldy method or that its justification and value are not appreciated.

5

Current approaches

Throughout this monograph emphasis has been laid on looking at and noticing the sequences of letters in order that we perceive and retain the percept in the interests of free spontaneous creative writing. This, as we have seen, is achieved through the exploitation of sight.

This sensory channel is indeed exploited on every hand, and reinforced wherever we turn, for we are assailed with visual verbal stimuli. In the past few neon signs excited us and advertisements were sober and informative. The village inn, once distinguished only by the life-size wooden fox chased along the wall by life-size hounds, is now clearly labelled with 'Fox and Hounds' and the brewer's name. Towns and villages are named with unmistakable clarity as one approaches them in cars that no longer bear merely the cryptic sign of the leaping Jaguar. Now they are clearly named Montrose, Princess, and even described with the single terse qualification, overdrive. But it is in advertising that we are most bombarded. Publicity agents no longer present vague muddled descriptive advertising, but stark names and startling slogans, and these appear most arrestingly and repetitively in commercial television. The reading level of TV advertising is about seven to eight years; the lightning episodes are often as appealing and dramatic to the five- to seven-year-old as the domestic and familiar episodes they are invited to listen to or watch with mother. Indeed, young children have been observed to stop playing and look up with eager interest when advertisements appear. But the stimulus to learning is in the fact that these short, neat, simple phrases are not only repeated aurally, but thrown simultaneously on to the screen. 'Eat yourself fitter' we are advised and told firmly 'You'll never put a better bit of butter on your knife'. The word 'bold' is projected as a flash-card on to the screen for three seconds at a time. All the technical skill and artifices of films, cartoons and television are tapped to provide intensity, change, size, repetition in the stimuli and to appeal to our basic needs of ascendancy, hunger, sex, maternal feeling, acquisitiveness. The words and names are not only presented in an inviting situation but also fulfil the demands made by the laws of learning, repetition, spaced learning, presentation in two sensory modalities simultaneously. Finally, television being so highly compulsive, children are well motivated to watch, and they focus, particularly in a poorly lighted room, directly on to the screen. Conditions are perfect for indirect reinforcement of word structure.

Exploiting the visual media

Children who have failed to learn to spell are likely to be children who have never succumbed to verbal stimuli visually. For such children this incidental tool of teaching, this fire-side visual aid, can be deliberately exploited, and in the home, the anxious parents can usefully encourage their children to catch spelling. The technique is the same as with a personal dictionary. The word must be perceived and retained. Again active self-testing must occur. The word or the phrase must be written from memory, without looking up in the middle, and checked when the word or phrase is repeated on the screen. Parents will frequently co-operate by checking. It is sometimes objected that trade names are unusual, and even incorrect. In fact very few of the 'Kleen-ee-zee' variety appear in television advertising, and it is the habit of looking and noting that is important, not learning to spell a particular trade-name.

This is a technique preparatory to, and essential in the

'caught not taught' art, that is, in the cause of 'incidental learning'. If the incorrect word is learned, this will be in conjunction with, and only apply to the product, and not the familiar word, which will have to be taught and pigeon-holed separately. What, anyway, are product names like 'Sensotronic' or 'Jeepers' for although nonsense in our own language, they do follow the rules and precedents of our own language?

Learning to spell by computers

With the proliferation of computers in homes and schools it is inevitable that spelling programmes are appearing on all sides. As with publishers' materials it is crucial that we examine very carefully the principles underlying any spelling programme in order to develop economical and effective learning strategies.

Since good spelling depends so largely on visual reference, the computer can obviously be exploited in the cause of learning to spell. Unfortunately there has been considerable commercial software which is not educationally or psychologically based, where, for example, a word is spelled out letter by letter.

If on the other hand the computer tells the child to look carefully at letter strings displayed on the screen, tells the child to identify these within words, and tells him to type out on the computer from *memory* the word he has identified, we are capitalising on the computer to the full. A good programme of this kind is 'An Eye for Spelling' (Cripps, 1984).

There is also a small computer called 'Helpspell' (Weyfringe 1983) designed to follow the Look-Cover-Write-Check routine with the machine doing all but the writing. The machine displays the word allowing the pupil to LOOK at it. The display disappears, thus COVERING the word. The child now keys in the word – this is the WRITING. If it is correct, the message 'Good – try another' is displayed. If incorrect, the child compares his attempt with the original and then repeats the procedure. This is the CHECKING.

Several problems arise in the use of computers for teaching spelling:

1 That a child will, if not monitored, key in a letter string letter by letter, so rehearsal of the letter string in one sequence must be insisted upon.
2 The child must be encouraged to transfer the words he has learned on the screen into handwriting.

Computers are here to stay and captivate. With their dominant visual reference and motor dependence, they tap the modalities crucial to learning to spell and they, if capitalised rationally, are even more than published materials a useful resource for teachers. But published materials increase in number and volume and it is important that such resources are evaluated.

Current materials

During the last two decades, a wealth of spelling material has been published and teachers have found it even more difficult to select spelling material than to select a reading scheme.

The *Appraisal of Current Spelling Materials* (Peters and Cripps, 1983) published annually by the University of Reading Centre for the Teaching of Reading, is an attempt at a consumers' guide to such materials. It was started in the aftermath of the Bullock Report (1975) when, with the anxiety about the basic skills articulated in the Survey by H.M. Inspectors of Schools in Primary Education in England (1978), there was a surge of spelling materials from every publisher in the country.

As a consumer guide, it might be expected that a 'best buy' would be indicated, but this is not the purpose of the document. What it is doing is to describe and evaluate the publications so that teachers can select what they think is appropriate for their own classrooms. What the guide does provide is a device for teachers to question whatever materials they are using, to ask themselves whether they are themselves providing children with safe and efficient strategies of learning and whether what they are doing is economical in time. What they can also ask, which the authors of the consumers' guide are not in a position to ask, is 'Is it fun?'

An examination of current materials shows that they are no longer in the form of straightforward spelling lists, as was Schonell's well known 'Essential Spelling List' (1932), nor are they in the style of traditional English exercises. A *Spelling Word Power Laboratory* (Parker and Walker, 1966) had already appeared and then in 1975 came Blackwell's *Spelling Workshop* (Sadler and Page).

Kits of this kind, other than American publications, have not appeared in the UK since 1975. This is probably because of the initial cost, and though attractive, and considered to be motivationally appealing, they do not seem to produce better spelling than the more traditional spelling books. Boxed kits do indeed provide system and consistency and are a central feature of the classroom. Since the whole class can work at one kit, it is an economical 'buy', but is all the economy in time, organisation and cost at the expense of efficient spelling strategies?

Nevertheless, straightforward spelling books float increasingly from the presses. Twice as many materials are now in the form of books and sets of materials in the form of exercises, games and activities as were published before 1975, but significantly fewer word-lists are now being produced.

In spite of increasing costs of production and frugal capitation allowance in schools, three times as many publications now include expendable work books, with a corresponding increase in the importance of the child's independent control of his own learning. Some of these are very flimsy and of High Street bookstall appeal.

More than half of the authors present their rationale for word selection. What this implies is that nearly half apparently select wordlists subjectively. The evaluating of published material, as distinct from describing it, is what is most relevant to teachers' selection of materials. This states whether a strategy for learning is in fact laid down, how much emphasis is laid on writing, on visual perception of the form of words, and what provision is made for independent procedure by the child.

Predictably, most authors attempt to justify the presentation of their material. It is significant that only half the authors present a strategy for learning to spell, and this proportion has remained steady over the years. The implication here is that half the authors leave the children to work out strategies for themselves, which may well be the *ad hoc* and random procedures described earlier.

Since 1975 the proportion of authors encouraging children to write without copying intitially has trebled, but the small number who continue throughout the material to encourage writing without copying increases only slightly, and there is a decrease since 1975 in the emphasis on the importance of writing. Since we rarely need to spell other than when we write, this is a very unfortunate trend. Authors should remember Schonell's (1942) insistence that spelling must be 'firmly cemented in writing'.

Half the material invokes rules and most of the material avoids inconsistent letter strings, e.g. jumbled words, which it has already been shown is an appropriate activity for competent spellers, not for those who are learning to spell. There is a growing tendency for materials to emphasise groups of words that look the same however they sound.

One particular current spelling approach which may appeal to the teaching style of some teachers is *Corrective Spelling through Morphographs* (Dixon and Engelmann, 1979). It is a way of looking at spelling structurally and lexically, morphographs being, for example, 'consign', 'resign' and 'signal'. This is what is usually termed 'lexical spelling'. That these are structural and not phonetic units will help the child to appreciate that one sound or phoneme in English can have many different spelling possibilities. It is a careful programme, but so far removed from the child's own productive writing that it is not of general value, which is unfortunate, since almost every word a child wants to write contains the morphographs listed in the book and there is much scope for generalisation.

The kind of structures listed as rigorously as morphographs and presented developmentally according to the NZCER list are *Catchwords* (Cripps, 1978). In the manual of this material are listed the most common letter patterns and the words containing them occur, e.g. 'wor' as in 'world', 'work', 'worn', 'sword', etc. The principle of teaching words that look the same however they sound, and writing them without copying is paramount. Another similar publication, *Spellmaster* (Bell, 1981) has the added flexibility within the classroom since it is in Pressure-Fax form.

These publications are not ends in themselves. They only support the teacher in her work of making the children aware of what sequences of letters are acceptable in English, of making them sensitive to the code, in other words, teaching them to 'catch spelling'.

Publishers are not helping the teaching of spelling by floating from their presses flimsy, filling-in, dot-to-dot, wet playtime books purporting to be spelling books. These do indeed occupy children, but that is about all. For publications to be effective, they must be seen as a resource, the contents of which support the teacher's approach to spelling and her taught strategies. For it is the behaviour of the teacher in the classroom that determines whether children learn to spell, and not books, materials and computer programmes. These can only support the teacher in her work.

What worries teachers more even than what materials to use and how to teach spelling, is how to deal with corrections and teachers' current approaches to correction technique must now be considered.

Correction procedures

In the classroom, teachers continually receive written work containing spelling errors and they are inevitably worried about the extent to which they should correct these. It goes without saying that 'write the corrections out three times' is a very uneconomical strategy. Instead, the teacher should be concerned about the quality *not* the quantity of errors. For example, when a child wrote 'Dad sed waht wood you like to do?' the teacher selected only one word for correction and the word she chose was 'waht'! This was because this particular mis-spelling did not conform to an English spelling pattern, and knowledge of letter patterns is essential in spelling. If the child had written 'wot' it would be a more acceptable offering than 'waht' because of words like 'lot', 'rot' and 'spot'.

The teacher ignored for the moment 'sed' as she saw this as an acceptable alternative according to the coding system. She ignored 'wood' which is not only an acceptable alternative, but also a homophone and depends for its correctness on meaning and grammar. She made a mental, if not actual, note of these words to be taught *on a different occasion*. Then she would teach 'said' as a word like 'sail' or 'paid, afraid'. It is so easy to accuse a child of not being a good speller just because he has spelled 'would' as 'wood'. This is a mistake that just *cannot* be corrected by 'writing it out three times'. It can only be corrected through experiences in using it. This was a thoughtful, rational and fruitful correction procedure, and there are many such.

In the following example of a six-year-old's writing the teacher wrote at the bottom 'Learn the word bought'. Even if the child could read her instruction, did he have strategy to learn it?

It is my brothers Burthday to day and I bouthe him a pensel and sone wone bouthe him an xylophone and some one bouthe him an clock whith some figas and He had some cards

'Learn the word bought'!

One way to deal with this is to concentrate on the 'hard spot' within the word 'bought' and write the sequence 'ough' above the sequence 'outhe' which the child has written. Another practical way of dealing with this is to tell the child to underline words he knows to be wrong. She then writes them in the margin for the child and rubs out the mis-spelling. She tells the child to look at the word in the margin, cover it and write it in.

This emphasises the need to highlight *where* the mistake occurs and provide the correct letter structure. For example, if a child writes 'women' as 'wimen' then the teacher would underline the 'ime' and write 'ome' above it. By correcting mis-spellings in this way, the teacher is enticing the child into *looking at* the 'hard spot' within the word. The wise teacher would also encourage the child to make use of the class word bank to look at other words which contain the same letter pattern. For example, 'home, come, some', etc.

Another rational way of dealing with this is for the teacher to rub out the words *she thinks are important* and write these in the left margin (unless the child is left-handed when she would write them in the right margin, so that he could cover over the word with his right finger). She might choose to teach 'birthday', a common and important word to a child, 'bought' in which the child was consistent in his mis-spelling, 'one' a much needed word of high frequency, 'with' a common and frequently mis-spelled word. She might ignore for the present less common words like 'pencil' and 'figures'. The child looks at her version on the left, covers it with his left finger, writes it in the space and checks it.

birthday   It is my brother's _____

bought   today and I _____

one   him a pensel and some _____

     _____ him a xylophone (asked for word)

with   and some one _____ him a

     clock _____ some figas.

The words learned are put in his word book or card index.

The following piece of writing, which can only be deciphered with difficulty, is transcribed by the teacher at the child's dictation. The nine words written correctly are put in an alphabetic card index. These are increased in number rapidly and the child helped to compose sentences using just these. It is limiting for the child but not as limiting as if he went on writing unreadable material.

> My nam is ——— I have 1 sast I like palleng on my bok I bas fond is pot gasin win I go hom fom pat bos nat by ham fan soll he das nat by atth to a tb and I go a vah the balor for a bat.

> My name is ——— I have 1 sister. I like playing on my bike. My best friend is Peter Jackson. When I go home Peter does not be out of school so I go for a ride round the Barlone until 20 to 4.

my	
on	
is	These are words he knows.
go	Begin with these in a file
have	and increase it rapidly
for	Only write these.
like	
and	
he	

Some of the most rational comments in correction techniques are those put forward concisely and systematically by Torbe (1977). 'The teacher's job,' he states, 'is not to correct mistakes the pupil has already made, but to help him not to make that mistake next time.' Torbe is quite clear that writing out errors a number of times is useless since repetitive copying does not involve the use of visual memory. He, too, strongly advises selecting the words to correct and teach, and relating corrections to what the teacher knows of the child's general approach to spelling. 'A teacher should be helper and guide', he writes, 'not a printer's proof reader!'

Of course the most important factor in correction procedures is *self*-correction and a useful basis for this is dictation. An unseen passage is dictated. The children are then asked to correct any words they think they have spelled incorrectly. The teacher then knows two things about the child's spelling. She knows the words the child thought looked wrong but more important than that she knows which words he does not see are wrong. She then, of course, teaches those words which the child does not know are wrong and which have clearly been overlearned in their wrong form.

A most valuable procedure followed by some teachers is to give a dictation regularly, a passage within the children's capability, and then instead of marking the errors, tick the words that are correct. The children count the ticks and keep their own record of their improvement in what is right, not what is wrong. These children see for themselves that they are on the way to becoming good spellers.

Some teachers underline incorrect spellings and tell children to 'look up' the spelling in a dictionary and learn it from the dictionary by the Look-Cover-Write-Check routine. But for this to happen, children must first be taught how to use a dictionary.

Dictionary techniques

The use of the dictionary increases as a child progresses through the junior school and again it is not always assumed that children need to be taught dictionary techniques. Finding a word in a dictionary in order to spell it is not the same as using a dictionary for word-meaning. In the first place the teacher must check that the child knows the sequence of the alphabet. The main problem is when the child does not know the first letter of the word he is looking up. This is again where the sound of the word does not help with spelling it. He wants to write 'sure', or 'chemist'. Words which provoke this kind of difficulty must be taught as groups of words with the same beginnings – sure, sugar, summer; chemist, chest, Christmas, church – and words with silent initial letters, sometimes called 'ghost words', e.g. knee, knife, knot, which must always be taught in collections. One interesting new dictionary (Thornhill, 1983) is a spelling dictionary which helps the writer with the initial 'morpho-graph'. If the writer wants the word 'launch' and looks up 'lor', he is directed to 'lau' or 'law'. Such systematic teaching of dictionary techniques are essential.

Many teachers worry that 'looking up' or 'asking' for words interrupts a child's writing. This may well be so, and some teachers overcome this by encouraging the child to

- (a) leave a space,
- (b) draw a light pencil line, or
- (c) write in the first letter, or
- (d) write any known feature of the word.

What is important to reiterate is that rote correction techniques of the 'Write each correction out three times' kind are useless. Indeed in the sample of children studied by the writer (1970) three-quarters of the children who made most progress in spelling were taught by teachers using rational correction procedures, while three-quarters of the children making least progress were taught by teachers using rote correction techniques. There are as many kinds of correction techniques as there are teachers. What is important is to remind oneself that techniques involving associating words that look the same however they sound, and a systematic routine of learning and self-correcting, is a rational and safe way into correction procedure.

Finally, it is crucial that the teacher does not correct fiercely every error that occurs. It is what the child writes not how he writes that ultimately matters. The content of what he has written must be first appreciated – and then the odd important and relevant word taught, lightly and incidentally, for correction procedures must always take place in a low key – a few at a time and always in relation to other words that look the same however they sound.

The way correction procedures are carried out will undoubtedly affect the child's image of himself as a speller.

The self-image in spelling

It is probably only when children are motivated to pay attention to the structures of a word, to retain the perception, to overlearn, to follow practices of active self-testing, to produce with pride a well-presented piece of work, that they are going to become good spellers. Motivation at such a rigorous level depends not on externally imposed incentives of immediate rewards (the prize) or long term success (advancement, status), not on the desire to conform, to communicate courteously, but on the self-image the individual has of himself as a good speller. Prescott Lecky (1945) turns to spelling as exemplifying human self-consistency. He quotes the intelligent poor speller, tutored ineffectively, his deficiency not due to lack of ability but to an active resistance which prevents him from learning how to spell in spite of extra instruction. 'The resistance arises from the fact that at some time in the past the suggestion that he is a poor speller was accepted and incorporated into his definition of himself, and is now an integral part of his total personality.' He must conform to this standard, must be 'true to himself'. 'If he defines himself as a poor speller', Lecky writes (p. 104), 'the misspelling of a certain proportion of the words which he uses becomes for him a moral issue. He misspells words for the same reason that he refuses to be a thief. That is, he must endeavour to behave in a manner consistent with his conception of himself.'

Such poor spellers maintain their standard of poor spelling. There is approximately the same number of errors on each page, yet, as Lecky points out, the spelling of a foreign language seems to be unimpaired, showing that the difficulty cannot be attributed to eye-movements, left-handedness or other mechanical interferences. In such cases the clinical technique which Lecky suggests, is to find strong values apparently unrelated to, in this case, spelling, which the student emulates, but which are inconsistent with poor spelling. For example, the student may like to think of himself as independent and self-reliant; yet the poor speller expects his defect to be condoned and treated indulgently. If the student can see the inconsistency here, Lecky suggests he will reject his definition of himself as a poor speller and determine to establish the opposite definition.

The moral for teachers is, of course, that, at all costs, children should be prevented from developing a self-image of themselves as bad spellers. For the child whose book or diary is fiercely corrected with red pencil, who experiences the insecurity of inadequate visual or rational reference, who is told to try first, but knows he will get it wrong, concludes 'I'm no good at spelling' and again his definition of himself is laid down and he proceeds to live up to it.

For this reason, many teachers do not correct errors in compositions in red pencil. Some rub out the error and let the child fill in the correct version from memory. For this reason, many present a system of reference, personal dictionaries or requests to the teacher, simple printed dictionaries, or lists of common words displayed. Words that have been written correctly are learned efficiently and economically with positive reinforcement. So methods of teaching both reading and spelling are designed to combine the best of all worlds, so that children can use visual reference, ('Lemme write it down and see if it's right'), possess some rational reference, so that, if they make an error, it is a logical and hence remediable one, and mnemonic, so that they gradually connect words that are visually similar with common words that are keys to less usual words.

Children who already possess this unfortunate self-image need the kind of clinical technique Lecky suggests for older people. They must be brought to see the inconsistency between themselves as independent or efficient, or precise, or courteous, and as poor spellers, re-defining themselves in terms not compatible with themselves as poor spellers. It is vital that children should never acquire a self-image of themselves as poor spellers, and to this end all possible help in the way of word-study and of visual and rational reference should be provided.

Techniques of study

One factor that has repeatedly appeared in research writings as conducive to good spelling ability, involves good techniques of study. In two investigations Gilbert and Gilbert (1942) showed that 'limiting study time may work to the advantage of the learner'. In investigation into the effects of teaching spelling through insistence on speed and accuracy of visual perception, they concluded that the most important task for the teacher was the proper marshalling of effort. Good techniques of study should involve finding the optimum study rate of pupils. Time spent on visual examination of the word should be limited, since they found that judicious training could effect an increase in rate and efficiency, and improve perceptual habits. They were quite clear that the practice of assigning words to be studied for an unlimited period was unprofitable and undesirable. Spelling should be taught, definite instructions being given as to how to learn, and should proceed as quickly as possible. In a study of eye-movements, Gilbert described one of the most efficient twelve-year-old spellers who, in the pre-test wrote 'definitely' as 'definitly'. In the subsequent learning of its spelling, however, her eye-movement record showed that she paid very little attention to the 'e' she had previously omitted. Another twelve-year-old, in learning to spell the word 'questionnaire', spent most of the learning period on the study of the word 'question' which she had spelled correctly in the pre-test. In spite of 'knowing' the word, she studied it! It is as long ago as 1919 that Horn advised us to test words before teaching. It was to avoid this kind of wasted time and effort in unnecessary learning that test-study rather than study-test methods were evolved (Fitzgerald, 1953). Freyberg (1960) advocates a positive approach to the teaching of spelling, a systematic approach demanding set word-study periods and autonomy of learning.

6

The assessment of spelling: how spelling is tested

If we want to know how good a child is at spelling, we can either look at his written work and see how many mistakes he makes (but the judgment we make is subjective) or use a normative test which measures how well the child is performing compared with other children of the same age.

In the first instance we are at most comparing his spelling with that of other children in his class who most probably are writing on other topics and using words of a different level of difficulty. So it has in the past been found necessary to standardise what he and the other children are writing and to do this eliminates for each child, not only his choice of the word he is to spell, but the use of that word in the child's own phrase and idiom. It also eliminates the mental set to 'get it down' in the context of the story he is writing and, most important of all, his own personal mental process from the idea to the imaged, perhaps articulated, written word.

The testing approach commonly assumed to approximate most nearly to this process has been dictation of the kind of words the children are most likely to need, but may mis-spell. But the teacher's pronunciation may be strange and she may enunciate the words indistinctly, so it is necessary to put the words in the framework of a sentence.

Even so the sentence has not the immediacy or the turn of the child's own phrase. The kind of sentences we use to incorporate e.g. the word 'breathe' (Schonell S.2. spelling norm 12+), 'We *breathe* the fresh air', has not the urgency that it has in five-year-old Fiona's sentence in her diary, 'I am a dragon. I breathe fire.' A sentence we may use to embed the word 'ground' (Schonell S.1. spelling norm 8+), 'Let us sit on the *ground*', has not the overtones of the nine-year-old's writing, 'The *ground* was slimy and moist and as I slivered down I found myself in a lovely garden where the snap dragons were dragons and flowers came to life'. though the word 'breathe' or 'ground' is equally clearly enunciated and the concept understood.

Normative spelling tests (recall)

Normative spelling tests are however the kind most used in schools. Schonell's Graded Spelling Test S.1. and S.2. (1932) consisting of ten words for each year, are such. The words are incorporated in sentences. This makes the test quicker to administer, but the norms are now very old. The words in Schonell's tests are 'first dictated, next embedded in an explanatory sentence and then dictated again'.

Another normative test in which the words have to be incorporated in sentences is Daniel and Diack's Graded Spelling Test (1958). This only gives norms up to 12.3 years, so does not cover the upper attainment levels even of the primary school. It is, however, very easy to mark and use diagnostically, since it separates in four lists words of different levels of use and spelling difficulty. A more recent standardised test is Vernon's Graded Word Spelling Test (1977). All these tests can be given as group tests, but with a wide range of ability it may be necessary to administer the whole test, many words being too easy for the best spellers, many being too difficult for the poorest spellers.

An alternative to dictating the words is to evoke the words by means of pictures and stories which are 'read together' (Lambert's *Seven Plus Assessment*, 1951). The norms here are for children from seven to eight. Fleming's *Kelvin Measurement of Spelling Ability* (1933) is a test in which the sentence dictated appears on the test-form with a blank for the child to write in the missing but dictated word. The norms are from seven to twelve years.

We would expect that this kind of test would be most valid. Yet this kind of test is a test of recall and we all know that it is harder to recall a word than to recognise it.

To be able to assess a child's knowledge of serial probability would indeed be a most useful way of assessing a child's spelling. This is a *criterion of spelling ability* and it is not derived from just knowing how one child compares in ability with another, which is what happens in standardised tests.

Such normative tests compare the performance of one child in spelling with the performance of other children of, around, his own age. The information such tests give is in the form of a spelling age which, for many reasons, is a very poor indication of a child's ability in spelling. We are told, for example, that a child has a spelling age of 8.6 years, whatever this may be thought to reveal. (It is hardly necessary to add that the whole concept of improvement in months which arises from normative testing is absurd in spelling.)

In other words, we have to ask whether spelling is a skill that the child is, or is not, on his way to acquiring. So instead of asking normative questions, e.g. 'Does this eight-year-old spell like other eight-year-olds?', we should be asking predictive questions. Without doubt the most important question we should ask is: 'Is this child on the way to becoming a good speller?' or, as Torbe (1977) asks, 'Is he a good or potentially good speller?' (that is only rarely makes mistakes, or can see afterwards that mis-spellings are wrong).

To know this, we need to know certain things about the child, possibly even before he has begun to read and write. We know that if any two of the four attributes most strongly predicting spelling competence (i.e. verbal intelligence, visual perception of word form, carefulness, speed of handwriting) apply to a child, he is likely to be a good speller.

To be able to assess a child's knowledge of serial probability would indeed be a most useful way of assessing a child's spelling. This is a *criterion of spelling ability* and it is not derived from just knowing how one child compares in ability with another, which is what happens in standardised tests.

Predictive information on spelling

It is, of course, much more important to be able to predict disability in spelling and the evidence is clear that if we know that a child is weak in verbal intelligence, has poor visual perception of word form (i.e. if he does not look at a word with interest, even if he cannot reproduce a bit of it in writing) and is generally careless, there is a danger that he will find spelling difficult. Indeed, if any two of these three conditions apply to a child, he is at risk in the area of spelling. So, instead of testing normatively, we should be asking if the child is verbally intelligent, if his visual perception of word form is adequate and if he is a careful child.

The third question, 'Is he a careful child?' makes us look at his general behaviour and ask where he comes on a grading scale, such as:

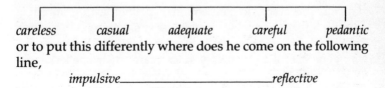

careless   *casual*   *adequate*   *careful*   *pedantic*
or to put this differently where does he come on the following line,

*impulsive*_____*reflective*

remembering that Kagan (1971) shows impulsivity to be a personality characteristic that modifies as a child grows older. It is certainly a characteristic that can be reduced by the teacher when she rewards any behaviour in the child that reveals thought, and ignores impulsive behaviour.

Again, we have noted that spelling demands in a child a certainty of attack, which stems from an habitual strategy. It demands a directness and purposefulness of attack on a word and a *set* to learn words as he meets them. 'The child', as Arvidson (1963 p. 20) says, 'should be encouraged to adopt a particularly determined attitude towards words that persistently give him trouble.' We can therefore add the questions: 'Is the child suitably *set* to learn words as he meets them?' and, most significant of all, 'Does he see himself as a good or poor speller?' This is a useful guide to the teacher, and significantly influences the child's attitude to spelling, since for later spelling success it is vital for a child to have a positive self-image as a good speller.

These questions are all designed to give information which is predictive of spelling ability, and are not tests of how a child stands in relation to children of his own age. They are guides to one's approach to the teaching of spelling rather than checks on what has been taught. Even at the pre-spelling stage, the teacher should be aware of the danger of the child acquiring a poor spelling self-image, and of the need for the child to be suitably set to look intently and intentionally at words as he meets them.

It will be remembered that Hartmann (1931) attributed spelling success to one special form of visual reaction which occurred in a flash-card situation and he suggested that to see how much a child could reproduce from a flash card in one glance is preferable to conventional spelling testing since it is so swift a form of testing. In the writer's research (1970) such flash-card presentation not only marked out good spellers, but was very useful predictively since many poor spellers were found to be able to see a word and reproduce it from memory, i.e. without copying. These children had just never been challenged to do this.

It certainly could be a method of screening children who might need to be provided with supplementary learning techniques, e.g. finger-tracing (Fernald, 1943). The kind of predictive and diagnostic question to ask here is: 'How much can the child "copy" as a result of one glance at a sentence, passage or flash card?'

As the word or words on each flash card are meaningful and within the child's reading ability and the exposure of the flash card is short, what the child has read is from minimal information, because he has not looked at every word, let alone every letter. He, therefore, has to reconstitute the word or passage mentally and it is this ability that is both predictive and diagnostic.

A positive assessment of spelling strategies

So far it has been argued that conventional (normative) spelling tests tell us too little about a child's spelling. Since spelling is an individual, all-or-nothing skill we should find out more about the strategy a particular child uses in spelling. To do this, we turn to the child's own free writing for evidence of his spelling ability. Obviously this cannot be standardised since what he writes is different from what anyone else writes. Nevertheless, the pattern of his errors can be examined and an error profile made.

It is hoped that this kind of analysis and study of the implications of what is found will impel teachers to look at their children's writing, particularly when the spelling is incorrect, with curiosity and not despair. It should give them guidance in the strategies a child is, or is not, using in spelling. The aim is that the child should learn to look at his own strategies and self-correct, so that he becomes autonomous in his learning.

If it is impracticable to obtain a child's free writing, diagnostic dictations for the three final years of the junior school in the writer's *Diagnosic and Remedial Spelling Manual* (Macmillan, 1979) can be used. The dictations are short stories of the kind a junior school child might write, but incorporating the most common sources of spelling error. Mis-spelt words are recorded and analysed according to whether the attempts are, or are not, possible in the light of spelling precedent, i.e. what can happen' or whether they reveal faulty auditory perception, inefficient handwriting or are just completely unclassifiable. This will identify children with glaring spelling faults and perceptual habits that are inimical to their spelling. Remedial suggestions are presented for dealing with each of these areas of difficulty.

Another good comprehensive *Diagnostic Spelling Test* was

published in 1982 by Vincent and Claydon. This was designed for identification and diagnosis of spelling difficulty in the age-range 7+ to 11+ and was standardised.

There are six very useful sub-tests:

1 *Homophones* The child making homophonic errors may have acquired the letter patterning of words, but is unable to link accurately pattern and meaning.
2 *Common words* This is a criterion-referenced test of words teachers expect the child to be able to spell.
3 *Proof reading* Good spellers are highly sensitive to written errors and able to correct them. In fact poor spellers can often identify words that do not 'look right'.
4 *Letter strings* This sub-test emphasises the importance of teaching groups of words that look the same, though sound differently, e.g. 'gone' and 'done' contain the same letter string but sound differently.
5 *Nonsense words* This sub-test indicates whether children have acquired serial probability, that is, know the common letter strings and the probability of these occurring in the English spelling system.
6 *Dictionary use* Dictionary skills, as was shown in Chapter 5, are important if children are to be autonomous in their writing and this sub-test provides a means of identifying children who need to develop these.
7 *Self-concept* This is not a test as such, but is very useful in assessing whether children see themselves as good spellers or have a dangerously destructive view of themselves as poor spellers.

A dictation is also included in order to examine 'how' a child spells by the analysis of errors and the flow of his handwriting.

Apart from Test 2 (Common words) and Test 6 (Dictionary use) all these sub-tests highlight children who have 'caught' spelling through visual experience with words, through linking the letter patterns of words (Test 1), recognising letter patterns that could not occur in English (Test 3 and 5) and generalising known letter strings (Test 4). These are not skills that have been deliberately taught, though a learning-to-spell strategy, such as Look-Cover-Write-Check, will, in fact, develop these abilities.

The other new test material of note is PRETOS (Proof Reading Tests of Spelling) (Croft *et al*, 1983) which is just what it says it is. It is standardised and, to some extent, bridges the gap between traditional achievement testing and the predictive techniques advocated by the writer. The authors warn that as these tests are designed to discriminate between pupils with differing levels of accomplishment, care must be taken when tests such as these are being used to provide information on the current status of groups of skills (criteria). By themselves, PRETOS would not be adequate measures of a classroom or school-wide proof-reading programme, or to provide diagnostic information for individuals or groups. It would be necessary, they say, to use some additional measures which sampled particular skills being emphasised in the programme being evaluated. In other words, PRETOS is too specific for general use. In any case, the skills of proof reading are not entirely the skills associated with good spelling; see page 90 where we are reminded by Torbe that proof reading is for the printer not a punishment for the writer.

It is hoped that the use of the kind of analysis described and the study of its implication in the case of particular children will result in teachers self-correcting their teaching strategies and becoming more flexible in their teaching. This is why there is no longer reliance on norms and, rather than direct pieces of prescriptive advice, only suggestions. The teacher, as a highly professional individual, is, and should be, autonomous. There is no single answer to the problem of all children's spelling. It is a mark of the professional teacher that he, or she, is prepared to tease out the answer to one child's problem at a time, for each spelling problem is unique.

Such diagnostic approaches should appeal to teachers who

are committed to being professional and to thinking about what they are doing. They are not a prescription for rule-followers. They are by no means definitive. Rather they are a challenge to the thinking teacher who sees his or her task as one requiring constant adaptation and intelligent self-correction of teaching behaviour.

7
Conclusion

In the last chapter it was shown that it is no good having tests which have developed in relation to all kinds of assumptions about spelling that are probably in no way justifiable. If one is going to have spelling tests at all, these must relate in some significant way to the determinants of good spelling and also to defensible methods of teaching spelling.

The determinants may well have been within the home and it is only to be expected that the younger the child the more the home environment affects spelling ability, but by the time the child is eleven, his spelling ability is determined more by the teaching which he experiences than by his home background.

In other words, a child who has not caught spelling has the opportunity in the junior or middle school of having it taught, and there is evidence that it is the teacher that determines whether he will, in fact, be a good speller by the time he is eleven. It is quite clear that progress in spelling occurs when teachers' attitudes are consistent, and when teachers are systematic in their teaching, when they provide safe strategies of learning. This shows too in the way they expect their children to correct their own mistakes – drawing attention, for example, to the 'hard spots' where the child has gone wrong, rather than demanding the traditional and ineffective routine 'Write each mistake out three times'.

So, whether spelling has been caught or taught, the fact remains that spelling arises in contact with parents and siblings who are themselves interested in word structure, teachers who enjoy playing with words, who relate unknown

105

words to the look of known words, teachers who themselves know what the spelling system is like. Above all, it shows in the confident expectation of the teacher that the child is on the way to becoming a good speller.

In the classic Scottish 'Studies in Spelling' (1961, p. 88) we were warned that we should pay more attention to the 'how' than to the 'what' in spelling. We were directed to the 'large share of research which has been directed to the content of the spelling lesson, the choice and grading of the words to be learned', to the *'neglect of method*, the development of efficient means of learning *how* to spell the words'. There followed in 1964 (Ahlstrom) and 1970 (Peters), the research already reported on the nature of the spelling skill, the factors that emerged in the two studies corroborating each other.

Word counts had already ceased to preoccupy research workers, and the publication of spelling materials did not begin to escalate till after the Bullock Report in 1975. This report certainly alerted teachers to the need for spelling to be taught in school to those who had not already 'caught' it if children were to be freed to write as adventurously as the report emphasised was desirable. Simultaneously, a body of research material was being collated on the nature of the spelling skill under the editorship of Frith, and this definitive text was published with the title *Cognitive Processes in Spelling* in 1980.

After considerations about the nature of the English spelling system it discusses how we deal with it, how we know when spelling is incorrect, and what happens, for example, when we read and miss incorrect spellings and as we vary our reading style to suit the text. But the sections of the book most relevant to the present work are concerned with factors related to how children spell. What the research suggests is that spelling is dependent on linguistic ability, the learning of letter sequences, and on visual imagery as a supportive rather than an integral component.

Frith has indeed drawn together wide-ranging strands of research on cognitive processes in spelling – but although we now know so much more about these elements 'until we know how to *alter* the cognitive state of learners', writes Marcel (1980), 'what is taught and how it is taught must be matched to the learner as he or she is.' It is with this that recent writers on spelling are concerning themselves. Torbe (1977), in particular, aims to encourage the right attitude to spelling in children and to match their needs with excellent specific and basic strategies. This is so also within the Research Brief for teachers prepared by the Centre for Educational Research and Development, University of Lancaster (1979). In a recent and relevant article which encapsulates much of what the writer is saying about the teaching of spelling, Pearce (1983) addresses himself to the teaching of the catching of spelling, to the learning of the letter patterns that are the conventions of English spelling, and to teachers' responsibilities and their caring, which occurs as long as teachers know the nature of the spelling system and as long as they trust it.

For it is ultimately to the classroom that we must turn. It is hoped that the implications of research will inspire teachers to look at spelling as a manageable skill necessary to children's freedom to write. That they are doing just this is evident in the many problems of school-based research with ensuing publication throughout the United Kingdom. Many arise out of in-service work. An example of this is the practical and personal statement by a teacher, Jo Fisher (1983). An informative booklet for parents arising out of work in school has been produced by Nichols (1978).

For it is now through school-focussed in-service work that teachers' former indifference to research in spelling is being transformed into enthusiasm about how to teach all children how to catch spelling swiftly and efficiently within an optimal learning time through writing, for it is only in writing that the skill of spelling is needed.

In the first edition of this book in 1967 adequate research was available for improving spelling instruction, but the problem of how to get teachers to apply the findings of research in their classrooms remained, as Marksheffel (1964, p. 182), had pointed out. In that first edition the following sentence occurred: 'The application of research findings will occur when the attitude of teachers to spelling is more positive. . . .' It is pleasing that now, sixteen years, and much in-service work later, this can be seen to be happening.

The application of research findings is occurring as the attitude of teachers to spelling has become more positive, and confident, with the result that the attitude of children themselves is such that what they 'catch' from the very beginning is a positive self-image about themselves as good spellers.

Bibliography

Ahlstrom, K. G. (1964), *Studies of Spelling*, Institute of Education, Uppsala University.

Albrow, K. H. (1972), *The English Writing System: Notes Towards a Description*, Longman for the Schools Council.

Andrews, R. (1964), *Research Study No. 9*, University of Queensland Papers, Faculty of Education, i, No. 4.

Arvidson, G. L. (1963), *Learning to Spell*, Wheaton.

Ayres, L. P. (1913), *The Spelling Vocabularies of Personal and Business Letters*, Russell Sage Foundation, New York.

Bell, P. (1981), *Spellmaster*, Holmes McDougall.

Bereiter, C. and Scardamalia, M. (in press), 'Children's Difficulties in Learning to Compose', in Nicholls, J. and Wells, G. (eds), *Contemporary Analyses in Education*, No. 1, Falmer Press, Lewes.

Bernard, A. M. (1961), 'An Experimental Study in Spelling', *Supplement to Scottish Educational Journal*, V (June 1931) described in *Studies in Spelling*, University of London Press, 1961.

Binns, R. A. (1980), 'A Technique for Developing Written Language', in Clark, M. M. and Glynn, T. (eds), *Reading and Writing for the Child with Difficulties*, Occ. Publ. (No. 8), *Educational Review* (University of Birmingham).

Bixler, H. (1940), *The Standard Elementary Spelling Scale*, Turner E. Smith & Co., Atlanta.

Bradley, L. (1981), 'The Organisation of Motor Patterns for Spelling: an Effective Remedial Strategy for Backward Readers', *Developmental Medicine and Child Neurology*, 23, 83–91.

Brazil, D. (1982), 'Kinds of English: Spoken, Written, Literary', in Stubbs, M. and Hillier, H. (eds), *Readings on Language, Schools and Classroom*, Methuen.

Breed, F. S. (1925), 'What Words Should Children Be Taught to Spell?' *Elementary School Journal*, xxvi, (1925), 118–31, 202–14, 292–306.

Bruner, J. S. and Harcourt, R. A. F. (1953), 'Going Beyond the Information Given', unpublished manuscript.

Bruner, J. S. *et al.* (1966), *Studies in Cognitive Growth*, Wiley.

Bibliography

Bryant, P. E. and Bradley, L. (1983), 'Psychological Strategies and the Development of Reading and Writing', in Martlew, M. (ed.), *The Psychology of Written Language*, Wiley.

Chomsky, C. (1970), 'Reading, Writing and Phonology', *Harvard Educational Review*, 40, ch. 2, p. 6A.

Clay, M. (1983), 'Getting a Theory of Writing' in *Explorations in the Development of Writing*, Kroll, B. M. and Wells, G. (eds), Wiley.

Cook, W. A. and O'Shea, M. V. (1914), *The Child and His Spelling*, Bobbs-Merrell, Indianapolis.

Cornman, O. P. (1902), *Spelling in the Elementary School*, Ginn, Boston.

Cripps, C. C. (1978), *Catchwords*, Harcourt Brace Jovanovich.

Cripps, C. C. (1983), *The Helpspell: Handbook to Computer*, Weyfringe.

Cripps, C. C. (1983), 'A Report of an Experiment to See whether Young Children can be Taught to Write from Memory', in *Remedial Education*, vol. 18, no. 1, February.

Cripps, C. C. (1984), *An Eye for Spelling*, computer programme, L.D.A.

Croft, C., Gilmore, A., Reid, N. and Jackson, P. (1983), *Proof-reading Test of Spelling*, New Zealand Council for Educational Research.

Daniels, J. G. and Diack, H. (1958), *The Standard Reading Tests*, Chatto & Windus.

Dean, J. (1968), *Reading Writing and Talking*, Black.

Diack, H. (1960), *Reading and the Psychology of Perception*, Peter Skinner Publishing Ltd.

Dixon, R. and Engelmann, S. (1979), *Corrective Spelling through Morphographs*, S.R.A.

Dodd, B. (1980), 'The Spelling Abilities of Profoundly Pre-lingually Deaf Children', in Frith, U. (ed.), *Cognitive Processes in Spelling*, Academic Press.

Douglas, J. W. B. (1964), *The Home and the School*, MacGibbon & Kee.

Education and Science, Department of (1975), *A Language for Life* (Bullock Report), London, HMSO.

Education and Science, Department of (1978), *Primary Education in England. A Survey by H.M. Inspectors of Schools*, London, HMSO.

Education and Science, Department of (1981) and others A.P.U., *Language Performance in Schools: Primary Survey Report No. 1*. London, HMSO.

Edwards, R. P. A. and Gibbon, V. (1964), *Words your Children Use*, Burke, London.

Ehri, L. C. (1980), 'The Development of Orthographic Images', in Frith, U. (ed.), *Cognitive Processes in Spelling*, Academic Press.

Eldridge, R. C. (1911), *Six Thousand Common English Words*, The Clement Press, Buffalo.

Fendrick, P. (1935), *Visual Characteristics of Poor Readers*, Contributions to Education, no. 656, New York Bureau of Publications.

Fernald, G. M. (1943), *Remedial Techniques in Basic School Subjects*, McGraw-Hill, New York.

Bibliography

Fisher, J. (1983), *Tackling Spelling*, The Educational Technology Department, Matlock College of High Education.

Fitzgerald, J. A. (1953), 'The Teaching of Spelling', *Elementary English*, xxx, 79–85.

Fleming, C. M. (1933), *Kelvin Measurement of Spelling Ability*, Robert Gibson & Sons, Glasgow.

Flesch, R. (1983), *Why Johnny Still Can't Read*, Harper & Row.

Foran, T. G. (1934), *The Psychology and Teaching of Spelling*, Catholic Education Press, Washington DC.

Freyberg, P. S. (1960), *Teaching Spelling to Juniors*, Macmillan.

Freyberg, P. S. (1964), 'A Comparison of Two Approaches to the Teaching of Spelling', *British Journal of Educational Pschology*, xxxiv, (1964), 178–86.

Fries, C. C. (1962), *Linguistics and Reading*, Holt, Rinehart & Winston.

Frith, U. (1980), 'Unexpected Spelling Problems', in Frith, U. (ed.), *Cognitive Processes in Spelling*, Academic Press.

Fulton, M. J. (1914), 'An Experiment in Teaching Spelling', *Pedagogical Seminary*, xxi, 287–9.

Gates, A. I. (1931), 'An Experimental Comparison in the Study-test and the Test-study Methods in Spelling', *Journal of Educational Psychology*, xxii, 1–19.

Gates, A. I. (1937), *Spelling Difficulties in 3876 Words*, New York Bureau of Publications Teachers' College, Columbia University.

Gates, A. I. and Chase, E. H. (1926), 'Methods and Theories of Learning to Spell Tested by Studies of Deaf Children', *Journal of Educational Psychology*, xvii, 289–300.

Gibson, E. J. and Levin, H. (1975), *The Psychology of Reading*, MIT Press.

Gilbert, L. C. (1935), 'Study of the Effect of Reading on Spelling', *Journal of Educational Research*, xxviii, 570–6.

Gilbert, L. C. and Gilbert, D. W. (1942), 'Training for Speed and Accuracy of Visual Perception in Learning to Spell', *California University Publications in Education*, VII, no. 5, 351–426.

Gimson, A. C. (1968), 'The Transmission of Language' in Quirk, C. R. (ed.), *The Use of English*, Longmans.

Graves, D. H. (1978), *Balance the Basics*, Paper on Research about Learning, Ford Foundation.

Graves, D. H. (1983), *Writing: Teachers and Children at Work*, Heinemann.

Graves, D. (1984), 'Patterns of Child Control in the Writing Process', in Cowie, H. (ed.), *The Development of Children's Imaginative Writing*, Croom Helm.

Greene, H. A. (1954), *The New Iowa Spelling Scale*, State University of Iowa, Bureau of Educational Research and Service.

Groff, P. J. (1961), 'The New Iowa Spelling Scale: How Phonetic is it?', *Elementary School Journal*, lxii, 46–9.

Groff, P. J. (1984), 'Word Familiarity and Spelling Difficulty', *Educational Research*, vol. 26, no. 1.

Bibliography

Hanna, P. R. and Moore, J. T. (1953), 'Spelling from Spoken Word to Written Symbol', *Elementary School Journal*, liii, 329–37.

Hanna, P. R., Hanna, J. S., Hodges, R. E. and Rudorf, E. H. (1966), *Phoneme-Grapheme Correspondences as Cues to Spelling Improvement*, Washington, DC, US Government Printing Office.

Hanna, P. R., Hodges, R. E. and Hanna, J. S. (1971), *Spelling Structure and Strategies*, Houghton Mifflin, Boston.

Hartmann G. W. (1931), 'The Relative Influence of Visual and Auditory Factors in Spelling Ability', *Journal of Educational Psychology*, xxii, 9, 691–9.

Hebb, D. O. (1968), 'Concerning Imagery', *Psychological Review*, vol. lxxv, no. 6, 466–77.

Higley, B. R. and Higley, B. M. (1936), 'An Effective Method of Learning to Spell', *Educational Research Bulletin*, xv, no. 9, Columbus-Ohio State University.

Hilderbrandt, E. (1923), 'The Psychological Analysis of Spelling', *Pedagogical Seminary*, xxx, 371–81.

Hildreth, G. H. (1953), 'Inter-Grade Comparisons of Word Frequencies in Children's Writing', *Journal of Educational Psychology*, xliv, 7, 429–35.

Hildreth, G. H. (1956), *Teaching Spelling*, Henry Holt, New York.

Horn, E. (1919), 'Principles of Method in Teaching Spelling as Derived from Scientific Investigation', in *National Society for the Study of Education 18th year book Part II*, Bloomington (Ill.), Public School Publishing Co., 52–77.

Horn, E. (1926) 'A Basic Writing Vocabulary: 10,000 Words Most Commonly Used in Writing', *Monographs in Education*, No. 4, University of Iowa.

Hotopf, N. (1980), 'Slips of the Pen', in Frith, U. (ed.), *Cognitive Processes in Spelling*, Academic Press.

Howes, D. H. and Solomon, R. L. (1951), 'Visual duration threshold as a function of word probability', *Journal of Experimental Psychology*, xli, 401–10.

Jarman, C. (1979), *The Development of Handwriting Skills*, Blackwell, Oxford.

James, W. (1892), *Talks to Teachers*, Longman Green & Co.

Jensen, A. R. (1962), 'Spelling Errors and the Serial Position Effect', *Journal of Educational Psychology*, liii, 105–9.

Johnston, L. W. (1950), 'One Hundred Words Most Often Mis-spelled by Children in the Elementary Grades', *Journal of Educational Research*, xliv, 154–5.

Jorm, A. F. (1983), *The Psychology of Reading and Spelling Disabilities*, Routledge & Kegan Paul.

Kagan, J. (1971), *Personality Development*, Harcourt Brace Jovanovich.

Kail, R. (1979), *The Development of Memory in Children*, W. H. Freeman, San Francisco.

Kamler, B. and Kilarr, F. (1983), 'Looking at What Children Can Do' in Kroll, B. and Wells, G. (eds), *Explorations in the Development of Writing*, Wiley.

Kyte, G. C. (1948), 'When Spelling Has Been Mastered in the Elementary School', *Journal of Educational Research*, xli, 47–53.

Bibliography

Lambert, C. M. (1951), *Seven Plus Assessment*, Northumberland Series, University of London Press.

Lancaster University: Centre for Educational Research & Development (1979), *The Teaching of Spelling: A Research Brief for Teachers*.

Lecky, P. (1945), *Self-consistency, A Theory of Personality*, Island Press, New York.

Luke, E. (1931), *The Teaching of Reading by the Sentence Method*, Methuen.

Luria, A. R. (1970), 'The Functional Organisation of the Brain', *Scientific American*, March 1970, 66–78.

Mackay, D., Thompson, B. and Schaub, P. (1978), *Breakthrough to Literacy Teachers' Manual*, Longman for the Schools Council.

McLeod, M. E. (1961), 'Rules in the Teaching of Spelling', in *Studies in Spelling*, University of London Press, 1961.

McNally, J. and Murray, W. (1968), *Key Words to Literacy*, School Master Publishing Company.

McShane, J. (1980), *Learning to Talk*, Cambridge University Press.

Marcel, T. (1980), 'Spelling and Language Disorders', in Frith, U. (ed.), *Cognitive Processes in Spelling*, Academic Press.

Marksheffel, N. D. (1964), 'Composition, Handwriting and Spelling', *Review of Educational Research*, xxxiv, 2 (1964), 182–3.

Martin, N. (1976), *Here, Now and Beyond*, Oxford University Press.

New Zealand Council for Educational Research (1963), *Alphabetical Spelling List*, Wheaton.

Nichols, R. (1978), *Helping your Child to Spell*, Centre for the Teaching of Reading, University of Reading.

Nisbet, S. D. (1941), 'The Scientific Investigation of Spelling Instruction in Scottish Schools', *British Journal of Educational Psychology*, xi, 150.

Parker, D. M. and Walker, F. R. (1966), *Spelling Word Power Laboratory*, S.R.A.

Patterson, A. C. (1961), 'A Review of Research in Spelling', in *Studies in Spelling*, University of London Press.

Pearce, J. (1983), 'On Teaching the Catching of Spelling', in *Education 3–13*, vol. 11, no. 1.

Peters, M. L. (1970), *Success in Spelling*, Cambridge Institute of Education.

Peters, M. L. (1979), *Diagnostic and Remedial Spelling Manual*, Macmillan.

Peters, M. L. and Cripps, C. C. (1978), *Word Bank Project*, Macmillan.

Peters, M. L. and Cripps, C. C. (1983), *Appraisal of Current Spelling Materials*, Centre for the Teaching of Reading, University of Reading.

Radaker, L. D. (1963), 'The Effect of Visual Imagery Upon Spelling Performance', *Journal of Educational Research*, vol 56, 370–2.

Reid, J. and Donaldson, M. (1979), *Letter Links*, Teachers' Resource Book 2, Holmes McDougall.

Rice, J. M. (1897), 'The Futility of the Spelling Grind', *Forum*, xxiii, 1897.

Rinsland, H. D. (1945), *A Basic Writing Vocabulary of Elementary School Children*, Macmillan, New York.

Bibliography

Russell, D. H. (1937), *Characteristics of Good and Poor Spellers*, Contributions to Education No. 727, Bureau of Publications, Columbia Teachers' College.

Sadler, B. R. and Page, E. G. (1975), *Spelling Workshop*, Blackwell.

Schonell, F. J. (1932), *Essentials in Teaching and Testing Spelling*, Macmillan.

Schonell, F. J. (1942), *Backwardness in the Basic Subjects*, Oliver & Boyd.

Scottish Council for Research in Education (1955), *Scottish Pupils' Spelling Book*, Parts I–V and *Teacher's Book*, University of London Press.

SCOTTISH COUNCIL FOR RESEARCH IN EDUCATION (1961), *Studies in Spelling*, University of London Press.

Simon, D. P. and Simon, H. A. (1973), 'Alternative Uses of Phonemic Information in Spelling', in *Review of Educational Research*, 43, 115–37.

Sloboda, J. A. (1980), 'Visual Imagery and Individual Difference in Spelling', in Frith, U. (ed.), *Cognitive Processes in Spelling*, Academic Press.

Smith, F. (1982), *Writing and the Writer*, Heinemann.

Spache, G. (1940), 'The Role of Visual Defects in Spelling and Reading Disabilities', *American Journal of Orthopsychiatry*, x, 229–37.

Stubbs, M. (1983), The Sociolinguistics of the English Writing System: or Why Children aren't Adults', in Stubbs, M. and Hillier, H. (eds), *Readings on Language, Schools and Classrooms*, Methuen.

Templin, M. C. (1954), 'Phonic Knowledge and its Relation to the Spelling and Reading Achievement of 4th grade Pupils', *Journal of Educational Research*, xlvii, 441–54.

Tenney, V. J. (1980), 'Visual Factors in Spelling', in Frith, U. (ed.), *Cognitive Processes in Spelling*, Academic Press.

Thomas, V. (1982), *Learning to Spell*, Curriculum Services Unit, Education Department of Victoria.

Thomassen, A. J. W. M. and Teulings, H. H. M. (1983), 'The Development of Handwriting', in Martlew, M. (ed.), *The Psychology of Written Language*, Wiley.

Thompson, R. S. (1930), *Effectiveness of Modern Spelling Instruction*, Contributions to Education, no. 436, Teachers' College, New York.

Thorndike, E. L. (1921), *The Teacher's Word Book*, Teacher's College, Columbia University.

Thorndike, E. L. and Lorge, I. (1944), *The Teacher's Word Book*, 3rd edn, Bureau of Publications, Teacher's College, Columbia University.

Thornhill, P. (1983), *Spelling*, Hodder & Stoughton.

Torbe, M. (1977), *Teaching Spelling*, Ward Lock Educational.

Townsend, A. (1947), 'An Investigation of Certain Relationships of Spelling with Reading and Academic Aptitude', *Journal of Educational Research*, xl, 465–71.

Trudgill, P. (1983), 'Standard and Nonstandard Dialects of English in the United Kingdom: Problems and Policies', in Stubbs, M. and Hillier, H. (eds), *Readings on Language, Schools and Classrooms*, Methuen.

Vallins, G. H. revised by Scragg, D. G. (1965), *Spelling*, Deutsch.

Bibliography

Vernon, P. E. (1977), *Graded Word Spelling Test*, Hodder & Stoughton.

Vincent, D. and Claydon, J, (1982), *Diagnostic Spelling Test*, NFER/Nelson.

Wallach, M. A. (1963), 'Perceptual Recognition of Approximations to English in Relation to Spelling Achievement', *Journal of Educational Psychology*, civ, 57–62.

Wallin, J. E. W. (1910), 'Has the Drill become Obsolescent?' *Journal of Educational Psychology*, I, 200–13.

Washburne, C. (1923), 'A Spelling Curriculum Based on Research', *Elementary School Journal*, xxiii, 751–62.

Watson, A. (1935), *Experimental Studies in the Psychology and Pedagogy of Spelling*, *Contributions to Education*, no. 638, Teachers' College, Columbia.

Wells, G. (1981), *Learning through Interaction*, Cambridge University Press.

Wheat, L. B. (1932), 'Four Spelling Rules', *Elementary School Journal*, xxxii, 697–706.

Williamson, L. and Wooden, S. L. (1980), *Facets of English Spelling*, New Mexico State University, ED. 195, 940 (Microfiche).

Woodworth, R. S. and Schlosberg, H. (1955), *Experimental Psychology*, Methuen.

Index of names

116

Index of names

Subject index

accent, 34, 35
ad hoc learning, 71, 85
adult illiterates, 4
advertisements, 24, 39, 73, 80, 81
alphabetic letter names, 66, 71, 72
articulation, 8, 15, 22, 74, 75
attending to detail, 20, 23, 24, 34, 35, 39
attending to skill, 14, 43
attitudes to spelling: children's, 47, 99, 107, 108; teachers', 1, 105, 107, 108
auditory dependence, 8, 20, 28–9, 47
auditory elements, 49, 74, 75
autonomy: in learning, 95, 101; in teaching, 103

Breakthrough to Literacy, 56, 57, 63

circumlocution, 6, 62
computerised analysis, 78
computerised spelling teaching, 53, 82–3
communication, 3, 58–9
'conferencing', 57, 58, 59, 60, 61, 62, 67
consumer guide to materials, 83
copying, dangers of, 66, 85
correction procedures, 86–90, 92, 105
'creative writing', 2, 5, 6, 22, 64, 65
criterion reference tests, 98

diagnostic tests, 101–3
dictation, 90, 96, 101, 102
dictionaries: class, 63; individual, 63, 64, 81; techniques, 90–1, 102

discovery learning, 2

errors: 'good', 8, 21, 75; medial, 73; unstressed syllables, 72; teachers' preoccupation with, 65
eye-movements, 32, 69, 94

family order, 40
finger-tracing, 22, 35, 39, 100
football pools, 46

generalisation, 18, 20, 43, 44, 77, 103
grammar, 11, 12, 16, 75

habit, 3, 65
handwriting, 3, 21, 39, 53–7, 67, 74, 101; joined-up, 56
'hard spots', 43, 44, 49, 50, 87, 88, 105
hearing, defective, 28, 75
high frequency words, 88
homographs, 76
homophones, 12, 27, 28, 75–6, 102

imagery, 16, 25, 31, 33, 35, 37, 48–53, 67, 75, 106
impulsivity, 99
incidental learning, 12, 14, 43, 68, 73–4, 79
infant teachers, 52, 54, 55, 56, 57, 74
information processing load, 61, 62, 63
initiation by child, 38, 53, 58
in-service courses, 76, 107
intelligent poor spellers, 25–6, 39–40
intent, looking with, 37, 39, 42, 48, 52, 57, 63, 66